BERETS, BAGUETTES, AND BEYOND

CURIOUS HISTORIES OF FRANCE

MARGO LESTZ

BOO-TICKETY PUBLISHING, LONDON

ISBNs
Paperback: 978-0-9931371-9-8
E-Pub: 978-1-9993118-0-3
Mobi: 978-1-9993118-1-0

CONTENTS

INTRODUCTION

I love France and history, and nothing thrills me more than finding some little-known, or quirky bit of French history. I call these stories curious histories and I share them on my blog and in my books.

Berets, Baguettes, and Beyond is a collection of these curious histories which are all related in some way to items symbolic of France. This book is not meant to be a comprehensive tome on all things French. It's simply a selection of stories and histories that I found interesting. I hope you will like them too.

Happy Reading!

PART I: CLOTHING

BERETS TO CHANEL

When we see an image of someone in a beret wearing a striped shirt we immediately recognize it as the French stereotype. In this first part, we'll discover where this image originated and look into the history of these items of clothing. Then we'll end with a story about Coco Chanel, one of the most famous French designers, and a time when an Italian rival quite annoyed her.

BERETS, ONIONS, AND STEREOTYPES

WHAT DOES A FRENCHMAN LOOK LIKE?

*I*n the mid 1900s, if you had asked nearly any British person what a Frenchman looked like, you would have gotten this description: He wears a beret, and he rides a bike with onions hanging from the handlebars.

Today, most of us don't associate onions with the French, but we all immediately recognize the caricature of a French person by his jauntily placed beret. He seems to have exchanged his onions for a baguette and a bottle of wine, but the Frenchman of our imagination just wouldn't seem French without his trusty beret.

Do the French Really Wear Berets?

This little flat hat is the stereotypical French man's headgear in the same way that the American caricature wears a cowboy hat and the British one sports a bowler. These distinctive head coverings allow us to immediately identify the nationality of the wearer – usually in a humorous way.

But do the French really wear berets? Well, just like the cowboy hat and bowler mentioned above, the beret was historically worn only by certain groups or in certain areas. At various times it was donned by men in southern France, by artists, soldiers, manual laborers, and movie stars, but it has never been the head covering of choice on the streets of Paris.

Blame the Brits

So where did this idea of beret-wearing Frenchmen origi-nate? It seems to have taken root in British soil in the 1800s. From there it spread to other English-speaking countries, then on to the rest of the world.

But the British didn't just dream up this image. There was a very good reason they associated Frenchmen with berets – and onions. The French man wearing a beret, riding a bicycle and carrying onions was actually a fairly common sight all across the UK from the mid 1800s to the mid 1900s.

Berets and Onion Johnnies

These beret-wearing, onion-laden cyclists arrived in the UK every summer to peddle their wares. They came from the area around Roscoff, Brittany in northern France. This area was (and still is) known for its special pink onions. They were sweet, had a long storage life – and the British loved them.

As it happened, many of these onion-sellers were called Yann, a common Breton name, which is the equivalent of Jean in French and John in English. The British soon took to calling them "Onion Johnnies." The Johnnies didn't mind and happily adopted their new English nickname.

From 1828 until after World War II, thousands of these Bretons would sail to the UK every July. They would go door to door, wearing their berets and selling their onions. Then just before Christmas they would return to Brittany. Since the local Onion Johnny was the only contact that many Brits had with a Frenchman, they assumed that all Frenchmen wore berets.

Bonjour, my name is Johnny. I am just a typical French man wearing my beret and selling my onions.

THE ONION JOHNNY STORY

How did it come about that these Bretons descended on the UK every year? The Onion Johnny story begins in 1828 when Henri Ollivier had a bumper crop of onions to sell. The road to Paris was long and difficult and since the Bretons lived so near to the sea, it was easier for him to just sail across the Channel and try to sell his onions in the UK.

So Henri loaded up a boat with onions and three or four of his friends and set sail. The British immediately took a liking to those nice pink onions, and Henri and his pals came home with their pockets full of money. Soon everyone wanted in on this business venture.

All the would-be onion-sellers got together and organized themselves into companies. Each company had a boss who would go to the UK ahead of the others and rent a building (usually a barn or warehouse) to serve as an onion depot.

The others would follow in July along with the shipment of onions. The voyage to the UK by sail boat took from 18 to 48 hours depending on the winds, and it could be treacherous. One of the worst accidents happened in 1905 when the steamer "Hilda" sank near St. Malo. More than half of the 127 deaths were Onion Johnnies returning from their season in the UK. Despite the dangers, every year boatloads of Johnnies crossed the Channel to sell their onions.

When they reached the British shores, the Johnnies dispersed to their various onion depots. These buildings, which were scattered all across the UK, would be their working and living quarters for the next five months. They often slept on straw in the space they shared with their onions. When they had sold all the produce they had brought with them, another shipment would arrive.

Life in UK

It wasn't an easy life. Strings of onions were heavy and men could start the day with 60 to 100 pounds of onions strung over a pole carried on their shoulders. When bicycles were introduced in the 1930s, it made their work much easier and the bicycle became part of their image.

Every day except Sunday, the onion-sellers started their day by donning their beret, loading up their bicycle with onions and setting out on their sales route. They didn't go home for dinner until they had sold everything. The boss accounted for all onions and made sure the right amount of money came in. This led many Johnnies (especially the young boys who started working around the age of ten) to quote the price and then say, "And a penny for myself, please." The Johnnies would keep their same route every year and, using their Gallic charm they inspired loyalty in their customers.

Language

Like all good salesmen, the Onion Johnnies quickly learned to communicate with their clients. In the early days, many of them didn't speak French – they spoke Breton, a Celtic language which is related to the Cornish and Welsh languages. Thus, many Johnnies liked to work in Wales where they could communicate fairly easily with the locals. Others learned English and spoke it with the accent of the region in which their route was located.

Rise and Fall of the Onion Johnnies

In the early 1900s, there were Onion Johnnies selling their wares in almost every city, town and hamlet in the UK. From the three or four men who originally went over in 1828, their numbers had grown steadily. At the peak of the trade in 1929 when there were 1,400 Johnnies selling 9,000 tons of onions to the British. After the Great Depression, the trade fell off, and in 1934, only 400 Onion Johnnies and 3,000 tons of onions arrived in the UK. Today, Onion Johnnies are practically non-existent, and those in the UK who have a hankering for the pink Roscoff onions can order them online.

They Changed how the World Saw France

Even though the Onion Johnnies with their berets and bikes are no longer a part of the British landscape, their image lives on in the French stereotype. These hard-working men were just trying to make a living while wearing their regional headgear. They had no idea they were creating a beret-clad stereotype that would follow their countrymen for many years to come.

In 2004 Roscoff opened an Onion Johnnie Museum to honor this almost-forgotten profession. It's called *Maison des Johnnies et de l'Oignon* (House of Johnnies and of the Onion)

The town of Roscoff also holds an onion festival every August (*Fête de l'Oignon de Roscoff*)

THE BERET

A HAT WITH ATTITUDE

The French beret, that little pancake of a hat, has become the recognized symbol of all things French – at least among those outside of France. The traditional French beret is just a flat circular hat of felted wool with a little "tail" poking out the top. But stick one of these on anything and it automatically becomes French.

It certainly is a practical little hat. It's warm, waterproof, and can be tucked in your pocket when it's not needed. But it's much more than just a simple head covering. It's a statement and an attitude that adapts to anyone's personal style. This might explain why it has been worn by such diverse segments of society over the years. From shepherd to artist, soldier to film star, the beret has identified and conveyed the mood of its wearer.

Even though the beret has a strong association with France, it has been worn in many parts of the world throughout history, and the French don't claim to have invented it. In fact, they credit Noah (from the Bible) with its invention.

Noah's Ark

Supposedly, when he was floating around in his ark getting rained on, Noah noticed that the wool on the floor in the sheep pen had been trampled and turned into felt. He cut out a circle, put it on his head to keep his hair dry, and *voila!* The first beret.

Shepherds

In more modern times, it was the seventeenth-century shepherds in the French regions of Béarn and Basque who were responsible for the beret's popularization in France. They figured if the wool kept the sheep at a comfortable temperature in sun, wind, and rain, maybe it could do the same for them. It's said that they stuffed wool in their shoes to keep their feet warm and dry. They discovered that the compression of walking on it and the humidity from the wet ground (and perspiring feet) caused the fibers to cling together and turned the wool into felt. These early shepherds made their berets from the wool of their own sheep. But they weren't great hat makers and their head coverings were sometimes smelly and hairy.

Mass Production

Then in the early 1800s mass production of berets began and the flat caps became more standardized... and better smelling. The southwest of France already had a long history of textile production so it was only natural that this was the area in which production of the popular cap began.

The first beret factory started production in 1810 and others followed. In the early factories, the caps were still knitted by hand and the little "tail" on the top of the beret was the ends of the fibers. When they began to be machine knitted, there was no "tail" so, of course, it had to be added – because a "tail-less" beret just wouldn't be a beret.

By 1920 there were more than 20 beret-producing factories in the region. With thousands of berets being turned out, it seemed that all the local men were wearing them. Boys received their first beret at the age of ten and it was seen as a rite of passage into manhood.

Worker Berets

Thanks to Napoleon III, the flat cap became known as the Basque beret. The Emperor married Eugenie de Montijo, who adored Biarritz, and the couple built a villa there in which to spend their summers. When Napoleon saw that all the workers building his villa were wearing berets, he started calling them Basque berets and the name stuck.

As a result of industrialization, many laborers from the southwest moved to cities for work. They took their trusty headgear with them, and the Basque beret became recognized as a workman's cap. The Basque beret, however, is no different than a normal beret.

Artistic Berets

But it wasn't only for physical laborers. From the mid 1800s to the early 1900s, the Parisian artists of the Left Bank adopted the beret as part of their artistic image. Maybe they wanted to imitate the great artists of the past such as

Rembrandt, or maybe they just needed to keep their heads warm when they weren't able to pay the rent. Whatever the reason, artists such as Monet, Cezanne, Marie Laurencin, Picasso, and many others enjoyed wearing the beret and depicting it in their paintings. The little cap is now inextricably linked with the image of the artist.

Military Berets

In 1889, the French military adopted a large floppy beret as part of the uniform for their elite mountain infantry called the "Chasseurs Alpins." During the First World War, the British general in charge of the newly formed tank regiment saw these French caps as a solution to his problem: how the men could climb through the small hatch of the tanks without knocking their hats off. The beret was adopted as military headgear by many countries.

During the Nazi occupation of France, the beret was adopted by the French Resistance. No doubt, its military history made the choice significant.

Berets for Women

Traditionally, the beret was a man's hat, even though some women were sporting them as early as the 1800s. But the big change came in the 1930s when Coco Chanel, who was famous for taking comfortable men's clothing and adapting it for women, made the beret a fashion statement for the ladies. Then movie stars such as Greta Garbo and Brigitte Bardot wore them in films and the beret has remained a female fashion accessory ever since.

That's One Expressive Hat

It seems that the humble little beret can be worn by almost anyone and can be formed to fit any face or mood. You can wear it flat on top of your head, slanted to one side, with the fullness at the front or the back, or you can even pull it straight down to keep those ears warm. Wearing a beret can express your country roots, artistic flair, or fashion sense, and it especially suits those who like to show their individuality.

So whether you want to portray yourself as villain or hero, simpleton or intellectual, the beret can help you define your image. It's more than just a hat – it's a state of mind.

French Toast

Add a beret and anything becomes French

Note: What an English speaker might call "French toast" is called "pain perdu" (lost bread) in French.

THE STRIPED SHIRT

THE FRENCH SHOW THEIR STRIPES

*I*f you're looking to add a bit of "Frenchness" to your wardrobe, a blue and white striped knit shirt could just do the trick. It's a classic that anyone can wear. Whether you are male, female, young, or old the crisp stripes will add a dash of flair. While navy blue and white are the traditional colors, these comfortable shirts can be found with black, red, and other colored stripes as well.

Sailors

This French classic can trace its roots back to the navy. Before 1858 there was no prescribed uniform for low-ranking French sailors. The officers had uniforms, but the lowly seamen just wore whatever they had. However, many of them did wear the blue and white striped knit top which was already being worn as a workingman's undershirt. It was comfortable, practical, and kept the guys warm.

Then in 1858, the navy decided that French sailors needed to have an official uniform. And the striped undershirt became an integral part of it. The rules about it were very specific: It had to have 21 white stripes which were twice as large as the 20 or 21 indigo blue stripes. The three-quarter length sleeves had to have 15 white stripes and 14 or 15 blue ones. The shirts were long, reaching to the upper thighs, and doubled as undies (which weren't yet in regular use).

Name that Shirt

Breton Stripes – These shirts are sometimes called Breton stripes after the Brittany region of France. There was an important naval base in Brittany so there were lots of sailors running around in their undershirts.

But these shirts weren't only worn by sailors: many Breton men wore them to work in. The onion-sellers (Onion Johnnies) who sailed from Brittany to the UK wore them, and this helped to establish the stereotype of the Frenchman in a striped shirt.

Marinière – The striped shirt is also known as a *marinière*. This word has come to mean the horizontal striped shirt, but originally, the *marinière* referred to the shirt the sailors wore over their striped undergarment. It was a solid color and had a large wide collar that hung down the back.

Tricot rayé – Often this shirt is simply called a *tricot rayé* ("a striped knit"). The knit fabric was soft and stretchy so it was easy to work in.

Why Stripes?

Why did the navy adopt these striped shirts as part of their uniform? No one really knows. Perhaps the man in charge had a keen sense of style. One legend says that the 21 stripes represented each of Napoleon's victories. Another theory is that the stripes would make it easier to spot a sailor who had tumbled into the sea.

Coco Chanel

Coco Chanel often went to the seaside for holidays and was inspired by the navy uniforms that she saw. In 1917 she launched her "Navy Style" collection. People often think she popularized the stripe top in this collection, but it was actually the large collar of the shirt the sailors wore over their striped undershirt which caught her attention.

Coco never sold the striped tee shirts in her shop, and they didn't show up on the runway until Yves Saint Laurent featured them in his 1966 collection. But because Coco was a famous designer and there is a photo of her wearing a striped top, people assume that she included it in her fashion line.

At the time of the photo, it was not uncommon to see people at the seaside or in the country wearing these comfortable shirts. What Chanel did do, was to use the knit fabric (*tricot* in French) in some of her women's clothing. This soft, comfortable fabric had only been used in men's underwear until she got hold of it.

Modernism

In the 1920s modernism was all the rage, and these tee shirts with crisp clear stripes fit right in. They were especially popular among the artistic types. Pablo Picasso was often seen in one.

In the 1940s and 1950s the striped shirt had a resurgence. It was worn in the jazz clubs of Paris, and on the Riviera it adorned Brigitte Bardot. It has never gone out of style since.

From sailors to film stars to fashionistas, this classic striped shirt seems to look good on everyone. The stripes have never lost their appeal and continue to show up on the famous as well as the unknown. They are easy to wear, with their sea-going, holiday feel. But, most importantly, they add that little touch of *je ne sais quoi*.

You don't have to be French to look good in stripes!

COCO VS ELSA

BEST ENEMIES

*I*n the 1920s, artists from all over the world congregated in Paris. The atmosphere was charged with creativity and a synergy that spawned new ways of looking at everything. Right in the middle of this circle of free-thinking, avant-garde artists was Coco Chanel.

Coco and Newfangled Fashion

Today we think of Chanel fashions as classic, but at the time they were revolutionary. When most women were still laced up tight in their corsets, Coco wore trousers and soft knit tops: comfortable styles borrowed from men's closets.

Coco reveled in her role as the uncontested queen of modern fashion. She had the full support of all her artist friends, including Cocteau, Picasso, Dali, and many more.

There's a New Girl in Town

However, toward the end of the 1920s, a new designer rolled into town and gave Coco a run for her money. Her name was Elsa Schiaparelli. She was born in Italy and had lived in England, America, and now here she was in Paris pestering Coco.

Two Peas in a Pod

On a personal level, the two designers had a lot in common. They were both strong, independent women who had built their own careers and succeeded in a man's world. Although from very different backgrounds, they had both overcome lonely childhoods and abandonment.

Chalk and Cheese

But their styles were like chalk and cheese: they couldn't have been more different. Coco went for simple and elegant, while Elsa preferred outrageous, and eccentric. Coco's colors were muted, while Elsa's favorite hue was "shocking pink," a color Coco described as "a pink that sets the teeth on edge."

The Artists

By the 1930s the Parisian art scene had moved into the land of Surrealism where everything was distorted and dream-like. Dali was painting melting clocks and by comparison Coco's styles were looking terribly tame. Elsa's outrageous outfits, on the other hand, fit right in with Surrealism. She teamed up with Salvador Dali and Jean Cocteau to create designs for her clothing line.

Coco, who considered both of these artists as her friends and supporters, was crushed to think they would "betray" her by befriending her rival.

Hollywood

In 1931 Coco was thrilled to get a call from American film mogul Sam Goldwyn who had decided that Hollywood's stars were too vulgar. He wanted Coco to give them a bit of class by dressing them in elegant Chanel styles. What a relief to think that at least the Americans still had good taste! She relished the thought of leaving Paris and "that Italian" behind.

As it turned out, though, Coco's elegance didn't have enough oomph for the Hollywood stars and they refused to wear her dull dresses. However, the same celebs who had turned up their noses at Coco's designs loved Elsa's theatrical styles. Joan Crawford, Greta Garbo and Mae West became loyal Schiaparelli clients.

Adding Insult to Injury

To make matters worse for Coco, on 13 August 1934, *Time* magazine featured Elsa Schiaparelli on their cover. It was the first time a designer had been given that honor.

In 1936, another blow: Wallis Simpson, one of Coco's faithful customers, appeared in a major photo shoot to announce her marriage to the newly abdicated King of England – and, horror of horrors, she wore a Schiaparelli/Dali creation! The "Lobster Dress!"

Perfume

Elsa even followed Coco into the perfume business. Coco had put her name on a fragrance which she had simply called "Chanel No. 5." And she had designed the equally simple rectangular bottle it came in. When Elsa announced her perfume some years later, it was called "Shocking" and it came in a bottle modeled after Mae West's bust.

Best of Enemies

It's easy to see why the two designing women didn't get on. Coco called Elsa "that Italian" and Elsa called her "the seamstress."

One evening they found themselves at the same masked ball. They pretended to be friends, and Coco asked Elsa to dance – then she "accidentally" backed Elsa into a candle which set her costume alight.

Coco Wins

Both ladies closed down their businesses during World War II. After the war, everything had changed, and Elsa wasn't able to make a comeback. She faded out of the spotlight. The House of Schiaparelli closed in 1954, although it was recently revived in 2013.

After settling back in after the war, Coco released a new collection in conservative black and white. Europe took no notice – but the Americans did. When France saw that the Americans loved it, they took a second look and decided they loved it too. And Coco was back in business...

Fashion Advice:

Coco: A classic hat and a string of pearls will serve you well.

Elsa: Bugs make a nice accent. And *please* wear an imaginative hat... a shoe, for example!

PART II: FOOD AND DRINK

BREAD TO BUBBLY

*E*veryone loves to eat, but the French have turned it into an art. In this part we learn about a few of the foods associated with France.

Bread is a French staple, and first we'll take a look at some bread shapes: We'll find out why the baguette is long and thin, and why the croissant is curved - or not. Then we discover the origin of the word *restaurant*, and the history of that controversial specialty, *foie gras*. Finally, we unveil who really made champagne bubbly.

BAGUETTES

LEGENDS, LAWS, AND LENGTHY LOAVES

*W*hat could be more traditionally French than the baguette, that long slender loaf of bread that has become an instantly recognized symbol of France? At any hour of the day, on the streets of any village, town, or city, you are likely to see French people strolling along with one of these elongated loaves tucked under their arm. That's because this ubiquitous bread can accompany their breakfast, lunch, or dinner.

The word "baguette" simply means wand, baton, or stick and refers to the shape of the bread. This term became attached to the thin, round sticks of bread in the early twentieth century. But the baguette's history may go back much further.

No one knows exactly when or why this French loaf took on its current shape, but there are several stories, and even some laws that give us clues to the baguette's heritage.

The French Revolution

One patriotic tale explains the possible origin of the baguette (but not its shape) by linking it to the French Revolution. Lack of bread was the principal complaint from the people of Paris and it played a big part in the overthrow of the monarchy. Bread was the mainstay of the French diet and people were tired of watching the nobility eat copious amounts of fine white loaves while they faced food shortages and had to make do with bread that was barely edible.

Making sure everyone had quality daily bread was high on the revolutionary priority list. In 1793, the Convention (the post-Revolution government) made a law stating: *"Richness and poverty must both disappear from the government of equality. It will no longer make a bread of wheat for the rich and a bread of bran for the poor. All bakers will be held, under the penalty of imprisonment, to make only one type of bread: The Bread of Equality."*

Some might propose that since the baguette is enjoyed by rich and poor alike, it could have been this "Bread of Equality." It's a charming theory and a very French idea of *Liberty, Equality, and Fraternity*, but could this law truly have created the forerunner of our beloved baguette?

Napoleon Bonaparte

Or did Napoleon Bonaparte have something to do with it? Another story claims that Napoleon passed a law decreeing that bread for his soldiers should be made in long slender loaves of exact measurements to fit into a special pocket on their uniforms. Since those measurements were close to the size of a modern baguette, certain people think this might be when the bread first took on its current form. If this is true, perhaps we have Napoleon to thank for the shape of our daily baguette.

Paris Metro

Or was it the Paris Metro? A different anecdote affirms that when the metro system was being built in Paris, the workmen from different regions just couldn't get along and the overseer of the project was concerned about violence in the dark, underground tunnels. At that time, everyone carried a knife to cut their bread, so the supervisor went to the bakery to request loaves that didn't need to be cut. A loaf of bread was regulated by weight, so in order to make it thin enough to be easily torn, it ended up being long and slender. Considering this, we might owe our beloved baguette to rowdy metro workmen.

Whenever and for whatever reason the first wand-shaped breads appeared, by the mid 1800s in Paris, they were everywhere. But these weren't the French loaves that we see today. No, they were *baguettes on steroids*. Many foreign visitors marveled at the extraordinary lengths of the Parisian bread they saw.

They described loaves of bread 6 feet (2 meters) long being delivered by women carrying them stacked horizontally, like firewood, in a frame on their backs. Housemaids were on the streets at 6:00 in the morning carrying these long loaves home for their employer's breakfast. In the afternoon, young boys could be seen using these lengthy baguettes as pretend swords and engaging in mock battles before the bread made its way to the family table. One visitor remarked that in a restaurant, the baker came in and stacked loaves between 6 and 8 feet (2 to 2.5 meters) long in the corner like a bundle of sticks. Another describes the bread having to be laid on the dining table lengthwise because it was longer than the table was wide.

Bon Appétit! Hope you're hungry!

Those long breads that made such an impression on nineteenth-century tourists must have been the forerunner of today's more manageably sized baguette. The modern, shorter version seems to have come into being in the 1920s, when a law was passed prohibiting bakers from working between the hours of 10:00 p.m. and 4:00 a.m.

The thin shape was probably developed because it allowed the baguette to cook faster. The baker could start at 4:00 in the morning and the baguettes would be finished in time for the first customer's breakfast. It was during this time that the term "baguette" became associated with the slender loaves that are seen everywhere in France today.

Bread has always been important to the French, and for centuries, it was their main food source. Today, even though bread is an accompaniment to a meal instead of the main course, it still plays an important part in French life – and the most popular bread in France is the baguette. Since there are *boulangeries* (bakeries) everywhere in France, there's never an excuse for not having a nice crunchy baguette with every meal. And while you're walking home nibbling on the end of your baguette, you can ponder the French Revolution, Napoleon, and the Paris Metro... and be thankful that you're not trying to maneuver a 6 foot (2 meter) long loaf of bread down the street.

BREAD DELIVERY LADIES

LES PORTEUSES DE PAIN

*I*f you like bread, then when you're in France you probably stop by the *boulangerie*, or bakery, every day to buy a *baguette*, *croissant*, or one of the other tempting treats that you will find inside. But if you were a *bourgeois*, or wealthy, family in the nineteenth or early twentieth century you wouldn't need to. Your daily bread would be delivered before you even got out of bed. Oh, wouldn't it be wonderful to wake up to a nice fresh *croissant* or *pain au chocolat?* Yum! …But let's get back to our story…

The job of bread delivery usually fell to women who were called *les porteuses de pain*, which means bread delivery ladies (*pain* sounds like "pan" without pronouncing the "n" and has nothing to do with hurting). These ladies would start work about 5:00 in the morning or as soon as the bread came out of the oven. Some delivered the bread in baskets or wooden frames carried on their backs, while others carried it in large, specially designed aprons. The lucky ones worked for bakeries that provided pushcarts.

These hard-working women could have up to 300 clients. They had to memorize all of their addresses, their likes and dislikes, and the amount of bread they required. When they arrived at the client's home they often had to climb to the top floors loaded down with bread. Even though some of these buildings would have had elevators, the bread delivery ladies wouldn't have been permitted to use them. Elevators were only for residents – servants and service people were required to take the stairs.

Since the French were (and still are) quite fond of their bread, the *porteuse de pain* performed a very important service. (I wouldn't complain if one would show up at my door this morning.)

"*La Porteuse de Pain*" is also the title of a book written by Xavier de Mentépin. It started as a series in a newspaper in 1884 and tells the story of Jeanne Fortier, a young widow with two children who is wrongly accused of murder. She goes to prison for 20 years, and later in her life she becomes a *porteuse de pain*, a bread delivery woman. Of course, she has many adventures along the way, trying to track down her children, searching for the real murderer, etc. This popular story has been adapted for theatre, inspired six films made between 1906 and 1963, and became a television series in 1973.

CROISSANTS

The flaky, buttery croissant is just as French as a beret or a baguette, but its roots lie in a seventeenth-century Austrian battle.

Croissant Origin Legend

The legend of the croissant traces this pastry's ancestry back to the 1683 Battle of Vienna... The city was under siege. It had been surrounded by thousands of Ottoman soldiers for two months. Supplies and morale were running low. Messengers had been sent to neighboring countries begging for help. But as yet, there had been no response. The weary Viennese were just about to run up the white flag of surrender when a messenger arrived. Good news: The King of Poland was coming with an army of allied forces. If the Viennese could hold out for just a few more days they would be saved.

Meanwhile, outside the city, the Ottoman army had a new plan for breaking through Vienna's thick protective walls. They would tunnel under them, fill the trenches with gunpowder, and blow the walls to smithereens. They were shoveling away in the wee hours of morning when everyone was asleep. However, that was also the time when the city's bakers had to fire up their ovens to bake the city's daily bread from their last remaining bit of grain. As they were kneading their dough, they heard strange noises under their feet. They hurried to alert the authorities who were able to dig their own tunnels and intercept the gunpowder.

Finally, the king of Poland and his army of allied forces appeared on the horizon. They charged the Ottomans who fled the scene. The battle was won and Vienna was saved.

To commemorate the victory, and the role they played in saving their city, the bakers created a special pastry. They made it in a crescent moon shape which was the symbol on the Ottoman flag. It was to remind everyone of their victory. They called their creation *kipferl* which means crescent in the Austrian German language. These pastries would migrate to France and eventually become the *croissant* (the French word for crescent). But before we go to France, let's continue in Austria a bit longer.

Croissant and Coffee

It seems that crescent-shaped pastry wasn't the only thing inspired by the Ottoman Turks. Their army had come to Vienna planning to stay, and they had brought lots of provisions with them. When they fled, the soldiers who had saved the city got the spoils they left behind. Some of them took camels, others took carpets, but one soldier took bags full of unusual beans. This soldier had traveled in Turkey and knew exactly what he was getting. He opened Vienna's first coffee house.

Unfortunately, no one wanted to taste his strange, brown brew. To make it more appealing, he decided to pair it with a pastry. He asked a local baker for a little bread that would go well with the coffee and would make people want to try the new drink. The Turkish invasion was still fresh in everyone's memory and the baker suggested the little crescent-shaped *kipferl*. The coffee and *kipferl* combination was a winner, and this was the beginning of the now popular French breakfast of croissant and coffee.

Marie Antoinette Legend

The croissant's curious story continues with another legend concerning Marie Antoinette, the infamous Austrian queen. She was sent to France at the age of 14 to marry the future King, Louis XVI. The lonely young girl missed her homeland and asked the court bakers to make her the *kipferl* that she remembered from home. She introduced it to the court along with other little pastries from her homeland. Collectively, they became known as *viennoiserie*.

By the nineteenth century, the *kipferl* had taken up residency in France, but it was a far cry from the flaky pastry we know today. It was still the Austrian version: made of a heavy dough, similar to that of a brioche, but small and in the shape of a crescent.

Around 1837, two Austrians opened a Viennese bakery in Paris. At that time the crescent-shaped pastry was still called *kipferl*, and by mid-century it had become a popular bread in France. As it became more common, the name was changed from *kipferl* (the Austrian German word for crescent) to *croissant* (the French word for crescent). Toward the end of the nineteenth century, the croissant took on its now familiar, flaky form and was on its way to becoming a symbol of France.

Curved or Straight

With so much talk of crescents and the croissant being named for its curved shape, I couldn't help but wonder why all those buttery croissants that I had eaten in France were straight. Why weren't they curved like a crescent?

Well, that's an interesting story too... In the beginning, all croissants were made in a crescent shape, and they were all made with butter. Then in the middle of the nineteenth century, margarine was invented. It was cheaper than butter and had a longer shelf-life. It was the way of the future.

Thoroughly modern margarine began replacing butter in croissants. However, the French like full disclosure on what they are eating, so the bakers had to let people know what was in their croissants. They decided to make two different versions.

Thinking that margarine would make butter obsolete, croissants made with margarine were left in the traditional crescent shape, and croissants made with butter took on a straight form.

The curved croissant (made with margarine) is called a *croissant ordinaire* and is now less common than the straight one (made with butter). The French seem to prefer buttery croissants (as do I) and this is why, today, in France most croissants are not really in the shape of a *croissant*.

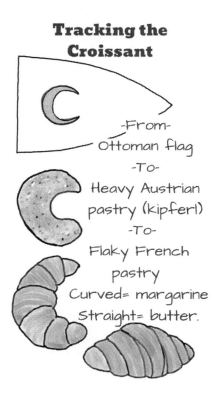

Tracking the Croissant

-From-
Ottoman flag
-To-
Heavy Austrian pastry (kipferl)
-To-
Flaky French pastry
Curved= margarine
Straight= butter.

THE RESTAURANT

MONSIEUR BOULANGER AND HIS RESTAURANTS

J'm not much of a cook, myself. My husband always says (only half-jokingly) that my favorite thing to make for dinner is reservations. If you are a fan of restaurants too, you might be interested to know how the word *restaurant* first came to be applied to a place that serves food.

Of course, there have always been places to eat outside one's own home, but they weren't always called restaurants. Legend has it that the first eating establishment to be called a restaurant was opened in Paris around 1765 by Monsieur Boulanger. In eighteenth-century Paris, there were a variety of places to eat, but they were strictly regulated by the guilds (associations of merchants) and each type of business had its own rules.

The type of food or drink that could be sold depended on the type of establishment: In an *auberge* a meal was served at a certain time of day, and the clients all sat around one big table and ate whatever the cook had decided to serve that day. The food was placed in the center and everyone served themselves. The *traiteurs* (caterers) sold stews, ragouts, and full pieces of meat which could be taken away or sometimes consumed on the premises.

Restaurant = A Healthy Soup

Then along came Monsieur Boulanger (whose name actually means "baker"). He specialized in restorative broths: thin soups that were thought to help people regain their health. These broths were called *restaurants* because of their restorative powers. In French the word for restore is *restaurer*.

Monsieur Boulanger's sign proclaimed: *Boulanger débite des restaurants divins*, or: "Boulanger sells divine restorative foods." Below that, another sign read: *Venez tous à moi, vous dont l'estomac crie misère, et je vous restaurerai*, or: "Come to me you whose stomach is suffering and I will restore you." He might have been making a reference to the Biblical verse in Matthew 11:28 which says, "Come unto me, all ye that labor and are heavy laden, and I will give you rest."

Restaurant = A Place to Eat

Eventually, the word "restaurant" which had referred to something akin to chicken noodle soup (good for what ails you) came to mean the place where these restorative soups were sold: Monsieur Boulanger's restaurant.

Boulanger, however, wasn't content to just sell his broths. He started to cook up and sell whatever he wanted. One day he went a bit too far when he served sheep's feet in a thick white sauce that seemed an awful lot like a stew. But he wasn't allowed to sell stews - they were the domain of the *traiteurs* (caterers).

The *traiteurs* took Monsieur Boulanger to court where he explained that he made his sauce separately on the side and only poured it over the sheep's feet after they had been cooked. In a stew, as everyone knows, all the ingredients are cooked together over a long period of time. Therefore, technically, his dish wasn't a stew. Who knows, maybe Monsieur B bribed the judge with a tasty plate of sheep's feet, but as the story goes, he won the case. Monsieur Boulanger got to continue selling his sheep's feet stew (I mean – just sheep's feet with a nice thick sauce).

Boulanger's Restaurant
-Eat when you want
-Sit at your own table

Today's Special

Sheep's Feet in separately cooked sauce

After that, there was no stopping Monsieur Boulanger. He made several innovations to his new restaurant. Unlike the auberges that served only at certain times, at Boulanger's restaurant you could eat whenever you wanted. And you could choose what you wanted to eat. He made up a menu and posted it at the door where people could see their choices and his low prices. He filled his space with small, individual tables instead of large communal ones. He even dressed up and stood on the street in front of his restaurant to coax people inside. His pretty wife helped him run the business, and this also brought in customers.

Monsieur Boulanger opened his restaurant in 1765, 24 years before the French Revolution. But it was after the Revolution that restaurants really began to spring up all over Paris. One contributing factor was that many aristocrats either went to the guillotine or left the country during the Revolution and their cooks were out of work. These former chefs to the rich went to work in restaurants and raised the overall quality of dining out in Paris.

History tells us that Monsieur Boulanger's first restaurant was located on the corner of Rue du Louvre (then known as Rue Pouille) and Rue Bailleul. Today that position is occupied by the Café du Musée which carries on the tradition by offering restorative light meals to weary tourists.

FOIE GRAS

*F*oie gras – doesn't that sound much nicer than "fatty liver?" But that's exactly what this controversial French delicacy is: fatty duck or goose liver. The controversy has to do with how the liver is fattened. Normally, the farmer puts a tube down the bird's throat and force-feeds him, a technique known as *gavage*.

France produces about 80% of the world's foie gras and the French gobble up most of that themselves. But they can't take credit (or blame) for coming up with the idea of force-feeding animals to fatten their liver. Humans have been doing this for thousands of years.

Egyptians

The Egyptians noticed that before geese (and other water-fowl) flew off on their annual migration, they ate a lot more than normal and got a bit chubby. When someone decided to have a goose dinner before the birds all flew away, they found that the liver was full of extra fat and tasted yummy.

They figured if they could make a goose eat extra amounts at other times, they could have a tasty fat liver whenever they wanted. So the Egyptians started force-feeding geese on a large scale. And they didn't stop there: They force-fed other animals such as cows and even hyenas.

Greeks and Romans

The practice of forcefully fattening animals passed to the Greeks and then to the Romans. They added more animals to the gavage list: They overfed pigs, dormice, and even snails.

Then someone discovered that they could add extra flavor to the fatty liver by force-feeding the geese with dried figs instead of grain. The fig-stuffed goose would then be given a dose of honeyed wine just before he was killed. This infused the fat liver with a nice, figgy flavor. In fact, the Latin word *ficatum* (which means "figgy") became the word for liver, and the French word *foie* is derived from that.

European Jews

When the Roman Empire came to an end, the foie gras tradition seems to have been carried on by European Jews. They used goose fat to cook their meat since butter and lard were forbidden under their dietary laws. Then around the sixteenth century, Renaissance chefs rediscovered the dainty dish and started buying their fatted goose livers from the Jews.

French Kings

Later foie gras became associated with the kings of France. The term "foyes gras" began to be used during the reign of Louis XIV, and the next Louis (Louis XV) served it at royal banquets. But it was under Louis XVI that it was proclaimed the "dish of kings." In 1778 the governor of Alsace served a special foie gras recipe to Louis XVI. He loved it so much he gave the governor a parcel of land in Picardie to show his appreciation. He also gave 20 gold coins to the chef who had prepared it.

After the Revolution (in which Louis XVI lost his head) regular people could enjoy yummy, fat duck livers and they began to show up on restaurant menus. Today most French people eat foie gras at least a few times a year. It's mainly served at Christmas and for special occasions.

Animal rights groups have protested the cruelty of gavage for years and a few farmers are starting to use gentler methods. But, cruel or not, fatty duck and goose liver is definitely part of France's culture. It was recognized as "part of the cultural and gastronomic heritage of France" in 2006 and is likely to be around for quite a while.

Honk if you hate foie gras!

CHAMPAGNE

WHO PUT THE BUBBLES IN THE BUBBLY?

*C*hampagne, that bubbly beverage that pops its cork for celebrations, is named after the region in northeast France where it's produced. The name "Champagne" is protected and only sparkling wine produced in the Champagne region can be called Champagne. The same goes for the process that assures those trademark bubbles: It's called the *méthode champenoise* and only Champagne-makers in Champagne can claim its use. But who really invented this method for ensuring that the wine sparkles...?

Dom Perignon

The people of France thought they had discovered the answer in 1821 when a Benedictine monk, Dom Groussard, told a wonderful story...

He told of Dom Perignon, a monk who had lived at the Abbey of Hautvillers more than 100 years earlier. He said Dom Perignon had experienced a happy accident when he opened a bottle of wine that had been bottled before it had completely fermented. The wine continued to ferment in the bottle, and when the monk went to open it, the cork popped out and the wine fizzed and sparkled. Curious, Dom Perignon poured himself a glass. He was thrilled with the taste and the little bubbles tickling his nose. He called out to the other monks, "Brothers, come quickly – I'm drinking stars!" Then Dom Perignon went on to develop a method of assuring that his wine was always fizzy.

It's a charming legend, and the French believed it for a long time. After all, a monk should be a pretty reliable source. But as it turned out, this one wasn't: He liked to exaggerate. Part of what he said was true: Dom Perignon did exist and he did work as a cellar-master at the Abbey of Hautvillers for most of his life. He was responsible for acquiring more vineyards and for improving the Abbey's non-sparkling wines. However, his work was documented, and there was no mention of him ever making sparkling wine, either accidentally or on purpose.

In fact, in Dom Perignon's time, wine with bubbles was something to be avoided. It did occur naturally from time to time and was called "devil's wine" or "pop-top wine" (*vin du diable* or *saute-bouchon*). The bubbles would develop when wine was bottled before the fermentation process had finished. Pressure would build inside the bottle and often cause either the cork to pop or the bottle to explode. Flying debris would hit other bottles and set off a chain reaction of popping and breaking bottles. This could cause substantial loss of wine, not to mention the wounds inflicted on any unsuspecting monk who happened to be working in the cellar at the time. So, while it's true that Dom Perignon did a lot to advance the Abbey's wine production, he never tried to create sparkling wine. In fact, he tried to avoid it.

It seems that Dom Groussard invented this story and embellished other tales to give the Abbey more historical importance. He also claimed that Dom Perignon was the first to use the cork and that he could identify which vineyard a grape had come from just by tasting it (both also untrue). But all of France believed his tale and gladly embraced the star-sipping monk as the inventor of Champagne.

It was a good story, and French business associations used it to promote the drink and the Champagne region. The legend also helped the reputation of the fizzy drink which had long been associated with royalty. Now that people knew it had been invented by a lowly monk, it would be a drink for everyone. In 1921 Moët and Chandon created a brand of Champagne called Dom Perignon after the monk credited with inventing the bubbly brew.

Carcasonne

Dom Perignon's newfound celebrity as the inventor of the Champagne-making process provoked another abbey in Carcasonne (southern France) to stick up their hand and say, "No, we were first." Benedictine monks in Carcasonne are documented as making a sparkling wine since 1531. Their version is called Blanquette de Limoux and is intentionally bottled before it has finished fermenting. So, while the Carcasonne abbey may have a claim to the first sparkling wine made on purpose, they did not invent the modern Champagne-making method. However, Carcassonne's claim gave rise to another legend which says that Dom Perignon had visited their abbey, saw their wine-making process and stole the recipe from them – it seems those monks were not to be trusted!

The British

Then in the 1990s, news came out of England that made the French Champagne industry pop its cork. Papers were discovered proving that the English were using the modern method of Champagne-making before Dom Perignon even entered the abbey. It seems that in the seventeenth century, England imported large quantities of non-sparkling wine from the Champagne region. The Brits bought it by the barrel, and bottled it themselves. They liked it when they got the occasional bubbly barrel and worked out a method to ensure their wine fizzed and sparkled.

In 1662 English scientist Christopher Merret wrote that "our wine-coopers of recent times add vast quantities of sugar and molasses to wines to make them drink brisk and sparkling." The British had an abundance of sugar from their Caribbean colonies and they added it to the finished wine when they bottled it to cause a second fermentation in the bottle. A great advantage for the Brits was that they had developed stronger, thicker glass that could withstand the pressure of the secondary in-bottle fermentation.

The method of double fermentation that the English used is now called the *méthode champenoise*. It was used in England from the seventeenth century, but the Champagne region didn't start to use it until the nineteenth century. Even so, the term *méthode champenoise* cannot be used to describe the process for making any sparkling wines other than those produced in the Champagne region of France.

So, while sparkling wine has occurred naturally and sporadically since people began making wine, it seems the method used in Champagne-making today began across the Channel in England. (Oh my!)

PART III: CULTURE

LANGUAGE, SUPERSTITION, AND INVENTION

*I*n this section we begin by looking at the language which plays a major part in French culture. It's so important that there's an organization in place to protect it from invasion by other cultures. Then we get a glimpse of some of the superstitions and curious customs that add a bit of color to French life. And finally, we take a quick peek at French inventiveness and discover a few of their innovations.

ACADÉMIE FRANÇAISE

THE ACADEMY OF IMMORTALS

*W*e English-speakers don't mind that our language is always changing. When a new idea or product comes on the scene, it's accompanied by new vocabulary. Whether those words become a lasting part of the English language or not, depends on how many people incorporate them into their daily speech. And no one is really bothered when new words appear and old ones fade away. We don't particularly care where words come from either. We'll take words from any language, as long as it helps us describe our world.

But not so in France. The French have an institution dedicated to preserving their language and keeping it safe from too much outside influence – especially from too much English influence. Since the English language is so flexible and accepting of change it has become the world's second language. France remembers a time when the French language held that title, and they are trying to hang on with dignity.

Académie Française

The *Académie Française* (French Academy) was created when the French language was at the height of its glory. In 1634 Cardinal Richelieu and a group of nine men interested in literature and the French language got together to create an institution "to give exact rules to the language, and to render it capable of treating the arts and sciences." And that's just what the *Académie Française* has tried to do all these years.

There was a short time during the French Revolution when the Academy closed their doors and hid away all their precious documents. But in 1803 Napoleon deemed that the Academy was neither political nor royal and restored the old institution.

The Academy is very prestigious but has no real power. The members publish the official French dictionary, *Dictionnaire de l'Académie Française* from time to time, and they give advice about the language. However, it is only advice and the government and the public can choose to ignore it (and they often do).

The Immortals

The 40 members of the Academy are all immortals (*les immortels*)! At least that's what they're called. They take this name from the Academy's motto, *À l'immortalité* (To Immortality) which was on the original charter.

Even though the members are actually only mere mortals, once elected, they hold their office for life. They can, however, resign or be dismissed for misconduct. (I wonder if using the wrong verb tense would count as misconduct?)

A large number of the members are writers, but that's not a requirement. Many other professions have been represented in the Academy such as politicians, historians, scientists, etc. Some of the more famous members were Voltaire, Victor Hugo, Alexandre Dumas fils, and Louis Pasteur.

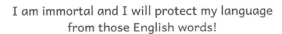

I am immortal and I will protect my language
from those English words!

How to Become an Immortal

The company of immortals is limited to 40. There are 40 numbered seats and candidates apply for a specific one. If there are two or more seats vacant, a candidate can apply for them separately.

The immortals vote to elect new members. The Protector of the Academy (the President of France) has to give his approval as well, although this is usually just a formality.

Then the new immortal is expected to give a nice speech praising the immortal who sat in the seat before him. If the new candidate doesn't, or didn't, like the person he is replacing, he must decide whether his desire to be a member of the Academy is stronger than his desire to belittle the previous immortal.

Eight days after the new member's first speech, there is a public reception where he makes another speech. This time he is expected to thank his colleagues for electing him. After all that, the new immortal should sit quietly in the meetings for one year before voicing his opinion.

Over the years there have been a few times when these immortals forgot their lofty status and acted as mere mortals, or more like children who didn't want to play nice together. In 1923 Georges de Porto-Riche was elected. But then he gave a speech that wasn't very flattering to his predecessor, so he never got his official reception. In 1918 Georges Clemenceau refused to go to his reception because he was afraid he would be received by Raymond Poincaré whom he hated. In 1958 Paul Morand, who had been charged with collaboration with the enemy after World War II, had his admission vetoed by President Charles de Gaulle. He was later granted admission in 1968, but de Gaulle refused to let him come to the Élysée Palace for a reception.

To date, there have been more than 700 immortals sitting in the Academy. Nine of them have been women. The first woman elected was Marguerite Yourcenar in 1980. As well as the nine women who were elected, 25 female candidates have applied unsuccessfully. The first woman submitted her application to the Academy in 1874.

The Green Garment

With a name like "the immortals," the members of the Academy really must have a special costume. And they do. It's called *l'habit vert* (green garment). It's a long black coat and a black, feathered bicorne hat reminiscent of Napoleon's. Both pieces are abundantly embroidered with green olive leaf motifs and are worn with black trousers or skirt. And if that doesn't make the immortals look distinguished enough, they also get a ceremonial sword to top off their outfit.

Oldsters

These cloak-wearing, sword-toting immortals are sometimes regarded as a group of oldsters trying to keep their language from changing with the times. In their role as guardians of the French language, it's not only the English words that they try to keep at bay. They don't like regional French dialects either. In 2008 the French Parliament was debating legal protection for regional dialects and the *Académie Française* stood against it. However, the Academy is making an effort to update its image and bring in younger people. In 2010 the Assembly voted that all new members must be younger than 75 years old.

Dictionary

One of the main tasks of the Academy is to produce the official French dictionary, the *Dictionnaire de l'Académie Française*. The Academy produced their first edition in

1694. It contained 18,000 words. But they accidentally left out one very important word. The immortals forgot the word *Français* (French). (Oops!)

During the first 300 or so years of their existence, the Academy has produced eight editions of their dictionary: first edition in 1694, second in 1781, third in 1740, fourth in 1762, fifth in 1798, sixth in 1835, seventh in 1879, and eighth in 1935. They are now hard at work on the ninth edition which they began in 1986.

I think I'm beginning to understand why they want to limit the acceptance of new words!

MAYDAY! MAYDAY!

THE FRENCH AND ENGLISH EXCHANGE WORDS

*W*hat does the month of May have to do with the call of distress? Nothing really, it's just an example of how words slip from one language into another. The distress call actually came from the French phrase, *m'aidez* which sounds similar to "mayday" and means "Help me" in French.

English is full of French words. That's because in 1066, William the Conqueror did what he was best known for and conquered England – and he just so happened to be a French-speaking man. For about 300 years, the language of the English court was French and all official documents were written in French. That's why today about one-third of English words are of French origin.

Languages are always evolving and the British and other English-speaking people have never been too bothered about foreign words cropping up in their own language. In fact, we rather welcome them.

Some French guy keeps shouting
"May Day" but it's October...

The French, on the other hand, are quite protective of their native tongue and the *Académie Française* tries to keep foreign words out. But, despite their best efforts, English words just keep popping up in the French language.

Some of them keep their English meaning, such as weekend, meeting, and shopping, but other words that sound familiar to English ears have a slightly different meaning in French. The French seem especially fond of taking English words that end in "ing" – and changing them into French nouns.

For example, in France:

You park your car in a *parking* (parking lot/car park)

You wash your hair with *shampooing* (which is pronounced something like shampwa)

To dry your hair you need a *brushing* (a blow-dry)

If you want a makeover, you get a *relooking*

To see if you are busy on a certain date, you check your *planning* (calendar/agenda)

If you are the sporty type, you put on your *baskets* (sport shoes) and your *sweat* (jogging suit – pronounced sweet) and go *footing* (jogging).

Sometimes however, just as we English-speakers do, the French interject a foreign word or phrase into their sentence just for the sake of sounding cool!

BREAD AND BAD LUCK

THE EXECUTIONER'S BREAD

*T*he French are a superstitious lot. They have many traditions that predict whether good or bad luck will follow a certain action.

One such superstition states that you should never lay bread on the table upside down. It's widely known that this action invites bad luck – maybe even the devil himself. But why? How could upside-down bread invite misfortune? What could be the reason behind this belief?

It seems that to find the answer, we have to look back to the Middle Ages when public executions were widely held. They would normally be scheduled at times when lots of people were out and about – on the morning of market days, for example. The idea was to show everyone what happened to people who broke the law, so the more people that saw it, the better.

The morning the example was being made, the executioner was a busy man. He would have to sharpen his axe, and make all the preparations. He wouldn't have time to stop by the bakery to pick up his daily baguette: that would have to wait until later.

The baker certainly didn't want the man with the axe to arrive and be turned away because he had sold all the bread, so he would turn a baguette – probably his best baguette – upside down. That meant that it wasn't for sale. It was reserved for the executioner and no one would touch it.

Don't even think about touching my bread!

The "man of death" was someone that no one wanted to have a chat with, so he would just walk into the bakery, take his upside-down loaf of bread, and be on his way. In fact, the executioner had the right to go into any shop and take as much he could hold in one hand. No payment required. And no one ever argued with him.

So, to get back to our superstition, laying bread upside down on your table was seen as inviting the executioner into your home, or by association, inviting in some kind of evil, or even the devil.

So, be careful with that bread!

MORE FRENCH SUPERSTITIONS

*A*re you superstitious? Do you avoid things reputed to bring bad luck even if you don't believe they will – just in case? Most cultures have their particular ideas about what is lucky or unlucky, and France is no exception. Some French superstitions are common in other places and some seem uniquely French. Which ones have you heard of?

Dog Poo

One of the strangest French superstitions, in my opinion, has to do with stepping in doggie doo. If this happens to you, your friend will excitedly ask, "Right or left?" That might seem like an odd question, but the answer is very important to your future. That's because if you step in it with your left foot, it's lucky! And, hopefully, the rest of your day will go better (after you get your shoe all cleaned up). However, if it's the right foot, you might as well just go home and pull the covers over your head, because the forecast for you is as stinky as your shoe.

Oh, lucky you !
It's your left foot !

Breaking White Glass

Another accident that at first might seem unfortunate is breaking something made of glass. But if it's white glass you are guaranteed to have good luck. *Verre blanc casé – Bonheur obligé.* And the more broken pieces the more luck you'll have. But if you're tempted to break something just to get some good luck going, I'm sorry to tell you, that won't work: the luck knows...

Table First

The importance of food in French life shows through in this superstition: When moving into a new home, make sure the first piece of furniture you bring through the door is your table. This infuses the home with good fortune (and gives you that all-important place to eat).

Just make sure you never have 13 diners at that table. If that ever happens, send one person to another room to eat by themselves so there will be only 12 at the table. Or call up a neighbor to come over and bring the number up to 14.

Salt

Spilling salt on the table is bad luck. In antiquity, salt was a precious commodity and essential for conserving food. It was even used as money, and the Romans paid salaries to their soldiers in salt. In fact, the word salary (*salaire* in French) comes from the Latin word *salarium* or "ration of salt." So with salt being so important and expensive no wonder it was bad luck to spill it.

Salt retained its importance during the Middle Ages and was heavily taxed. In Leonardo daVinci's painting "The Last Supper," Judas is depicted as spilling the salt. Today, people are no longer paid in salt, nor do they pay an extra tax on it, but the superstition persists. This is why in France you should never hand the salt to another person at the table. Just carefully set it near them and give them the responsibility of not spilling it. However, it is allowed to throw a pinch of salt over your shoulder to keep bad luck at bay.

Cheers

When making a toast and touching glasses, you must make eye contact with the other person. If not, you will be unlucky in love for seven years! Quite a hefty penalty! This superstition seems to come from the Middle Ages when slipping poison in someone's drink was not uncommon. The custom was to pour a bit of liquid from each glass into the other – just in case – and then to look straight into the eyes of the other person watching out for suspicious behavior.

Friday 13th

As in many places, Friday 13th is considered an unlucky day in general. Many people think it's a bad day to move house or start a new venture. However, it's considered a lucky day to buy lottery tickets. So, maybe you want to try your lotto luck on the next Friday 13th.

Clothes

There are a few superstitions concerning clothes. It's good luck to touch the red pompom on top of a sailor's hat. It's bad luck for actors to wear green during a performance – Molière is said to have died dressed in green just before going on stage. And it's bad luck to wear new clothes on a Friday (so save that new frock for Saturday).

Spiders

Finding a spider on your clothes means there is money coming your way. Spiders in general can predict good or bad luck. It all depends on when you see them. A French proverb says, *araignée du matin, chagrin – araignée du midi, souci – araignée du soir, espoir*. This means: "Spider in the morning, sadness – spider at mid-day, worry – spider in the evening, hope." This superstition seems to come from the spider's reputation as a weather predictor. If she is working early in the morning it means there was no dew to impede her, and if there was no dew that means rain is on the way (sadness). If the spider is working at midday, that also predicts rain (worry). And a spider taking her time weaving her web in the evening means no rain is in sight (hope).

If you see a spider spinning her web from top to bottom – expect some cash. If you kill a spider, it will bring you bad luck. But if you feel the spider's death is absolutely necessary, you should do the deed with the right foot and never in the morning.

Cats

A black cat crossing the street brings bad luck. It's said that Napoleon saw just such a sight right before the battle of Waterloo – and we all know that didn't go well for him. Never cross a stream holding a cat of any color. I can imagine that might be because most cats don't like to be held over water and he might leave you covered in scratches. If a cat sneezes near a bride on her wedding day, the marriage will be a happy one.

The Gift of a Knife

Giving a knife as a gift is seen as severing the ties of friendship, so if someone receives a knife, they give a small amount of money in return. This way it's not a gift and everyone is safe and can remain friends.

THREE USEFUL FRENCH INVENTIONS

We have so many modern conveniences, and we rarely stop to think about what life might have been like before they were invented, or give a thought to their inventor. Below we take a look at the history behind three French inventions that make our lives easier.

HAIR DRYER

You probably don't give much thought to your lowly little hair dryer. You just take it for granted that you can wash your hair, and have it completely dry in a matter of minutes. But that wasn't always the case.

Before the late 1800s you would have had to wait for nature to do the job – and when fashion dictated that ladies wore long thick tresses, that could have taken several hours. All that changed when the hair dryer was invented.

Alexandre Ferdinand Godefroy was a French man who called himself a hairstylist/inventor. This inventive hairstylist was living, and running a salon, in St. Louis, Missouri when he patented his newfangled invention in 1888.

Even though this contraption was a great leap forward in women's hair care, it was a far cry from the nifty little handheld electric blow dryers of today. It consisted of a large hood hooked up to a gas heater. Small pipes coming off the main flue directed hot air to various parts of the head, and a little chimney on top let the steam escape so it wouldn't scald the lady's head.

It must have been the talk of the town when Monsieur Godefroy installed his new "hair dressing device," as he called it, in his St. Louis salon. But those who didn't want to go to the salon to dry their hair didn't have long to wait for a do-it-yourself solution. When the electric vacuum cleaner was introduced, it was also marketed as a home hair dryer. It was a bit complicated: The vacuum exhaust pipe was connected to a box with a toaster inside. The toaster would warm the air in the box and another hose would direct the warm air current to the hair, and voila! A home hairdryer – how clever (and strange) is that?

Now, when you pick up your little blow dryer in the morning, maybe you'll have more appreciation for it – and its French inventor.

STETHOSCOPE

In the early 1800s, if you went to the doctor and he needed to listen to your heartbeat or your lungs he would simply lay his head on your chest and listen. That worked well most of the time, but it seems that Dr. René Laënnec was a religious and modest man. Pressing his ear to the chest of his young female patients just didn't seem quite proper.

One day he walked past a group of children playing near a construction site. He stopped to watch as a boy at one end of a wooden beam ran a pin across it. Children at the other end had their ears on the beam and were giggling in delight that the wood carried the sound of the pin all the way down to them.

This gave the shy doctor an idea, and next time a young woman came into his office with a heart complaint, he had the opportunity to test it. Normally, he would have gone ear to heart, despite his embarrassment – but not this time. Remembering the children he had seen, he rolled a sheet of paper into a tube and placed one end over the lady's chest and the other end in his ear. To his happy surprise, he heard her heart beat loud and clear. This led him to design a wooden version of what has now become a staple in every doctor's kit.

So, depending on your relationship with your doctor, you may or may not think the stethoscope is an improvement.

FOOD PRESERVATION

Some people (like me) just aren't cut out for cooking. If you're one of them, you'll appreciate that some things can be bought in jars and cans. Indirectly, we have Napoleon Bonaparte to thank for that.

Napoleon liked to go to war. He thought he might even be able to take over the whole world if he could only figure out how to feed all those soldiers. So he offered a cash prize to anyone who could come up with a method of conserving food that could be transported along with his army.

Nicolas Appert, a Parisian chef, won the money by boiling food inside sealed glass jars. No one understood why this kept the food from spoiling, because Louis Pasteur, another French man, hadn't yet discovered the role of microbes in food spoilage. But Nicolas' method worked and that was all that mattered.

He collected his 12,000 Francs prize money in 1810 and used it to set up a canning factory. Unfortunately for Nicolas, his factory was destroyed four years later, in 1814, when the other European countries had had enough of Napoleon's invasions. They all ganged up on him, marched into France, and drove him into exile – tearing down Nicolas' factory along the way.

While glass bottles did a good job of preserving food, they did have drawbacks - the main one being that they were breakable. Soon a method for preserving food in cans was invented, by another French man, Philippe de Girard. The cans were much more portable and useful for soldiers and sailors, and eventually, these canned foods found their way into modern kitchens everywhere.

So, the next time you open a can of tuna, go to the doctor, or dry your hair, remember these French inventors and what they did to make your life easier.

Of course, there are many other French inventions, such as the metric system, pasteurization, photography, the home refrigerator, braille, mayonnaise, the hot air balloon, and the pencil sharpener, just to name a few.

Thanks to a few clever French inventors

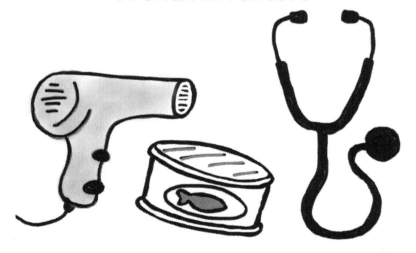

PART IV: SYMBOLS

ROOSTERS, FROGS, AND FLAGS

The rooster symbolizes France, and in this section, we find out more about the cockerel's connection with the country. Then we examine why the French are sometimes (affectionately or otherwise) called frogs and how these amphibians morphed into fleurs de lys. And, finally, we look at the blue, white, and red national flag.

THE GALLIC ROOSTER

*M*any nations are represented by the symbol of an animal. Normally, they choose one whose characteristics reflect those of the country: The United Kingdom chose the brave lion and the United States claims the majestic bald eagle. What animal do you think represents France? ... The barnyard rooster.

Of course, France has other symbols – such as Marianne, the tricolor flag, the national anthem, etc. But the oldest emblem of France is the Gallic rooster (or *le coq gaulois* in French). In fact, the rooster was used to represent the people of this region before they were even French.

Blame it on the Romans

To find out how this came about, we have to go all the way back to the Roman era when the area now known as France was part of Gaul. Gaul was a large region made up of modern-day France, Luxembourg, Belgium, most of

Switzerland, northern Italy, and bits of the Netherlands and Germany. It was inhabited by several Gallic tribes.

In 58 BC Rome and Gaul were "best enemies." They had been attacking each other for a few hundred years, and Julius Caesar was just about to put an end to it. He began the Gallic Wars to take over the land of Gaul.

It was the invading Romans who were responsible for making the barnyard bird the symbol of France. It seems that in Latin, the word *gallus* meant both "the people of Gaul" and "cockerel." The Romans had a good laugh at those "roosters" who were arrogant enough to stand up and crow at the imperial Roman eagle. So, they used the image of the rooster as a way to belittle and deride the people of Gaul.

But the Gauls were brave in battle and decided to adopt their feathered namesake as a symbol of courage – because roosters will fight to protect their flock and will take on any other animal no matter how big. The image of the Gallic rooster stuck. In the fifth century when the Romans disappeared and the Franks came along, the *coq gaulois* was already engrained in the culture.

Revolutionary Rooster

The cockerel began to officially represent the French nation during the Renaissance when the French kings used the bird's image to decorate official emblems and coins. But the humble rooster really had something to crow about when the French Revolution came along.

The cockerel was an animal of the people in a revolution of the people. The revolutionaries used his image to represented vigilance and hard work. He woke up the peasants when it was time to start their day's labor and he would alert them to any disturbances during the night. The red comb on top of his head made it seem as if he wore his own red Phrygian cap – the revolutionary red bonnet symbolizing liberty.

But then Napoleon came along and declared himself emperor. He knocked the rooster right off his roost and banished him from his role as representative of France. The Emperor claimed the cockerel was not strong and it was unworthy to represent such a great empire as France. In its place, he adopted the imperial eagle.

Modern French Rooster

In 1870 when the Third Republic was adopted, the rooster crowed, flapped his wings, and hopped back up on the roost where he has stayed ever since. He has been featured on postage stamps, coins, mayoral insignias, war propaganda, war memorials, etc. During the Second World War, he became a symbol of resistance, courage, and patriotism.

Why is it that the lowly *coq gaulois* has stood the test of time as a symbol of France? Did the Romans hit the nail on the head all those centuries ago? Does the rooster relate in some way to the French character? Are the French proud, boastful, and courageous like their feathered representative? Well, according to some people (not me, of course) the rooster is the perfect symbol for France because it's the only animal that still crows with pride even when he's standing in *la merde* (crap).

Today the cockerel is a minor symbol of the republic, but he's still going strong in the world of sports. France's national football team has worn shirts bearing a Gallic rooster for more than 100 years. They even have a live rooster mascot who attends all the games and inspires their cockiness.

And, in case you are wondering what French roosters say in the mornings – they shout *cocorico*, the French version of cockadoodledoo. "*Cocorico!*" is also an exclamation of national pride used whenever the French want to crow about some national victory or accomplishment.

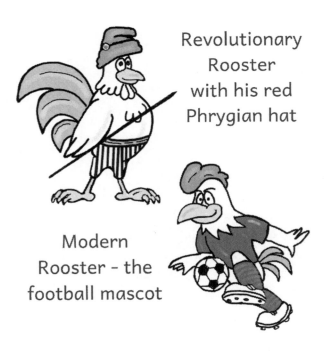

Revolutionary Rooster with his red Phrygian hat

Modern Rooster – the football mascot

RENART AND CHANTECLER

TWO ANIMALS THAT SHAPED FRENCH CULTURE AND LANGUAGE

*C*hantecler is a favored name for roosters in France. To find out why, we must first go back to the twelfth century and start with a fox. In those ancient days, minstrels traveled from town to town entertaining people with rhyming stories. And in medieval France, it seems that many of those stories had to do with a fox named Renart. Twenty-seven animal-centered fables, all written by different authors at different times, were assembled into an anthology called *Le Roman de Renart* (The Book of Renart).

These stories about Renart the fox and his interaction with other animals were updated throughout history and are still enjoyed by French children today. In one of the most popular tales, Renart had a run-in with a rooster whose name was Chantecler. But we'll talk about the rooster in a minute. First let's learn more about the fox.

Renart the Fox

If you speak French, you know that the French word for fox is *renard*. So, you might think that Renart (later spelled Renard) was given this name because he was a fox. But you would be wrong – it was the other way around: Renard is now the word for fox because of this particular character.

Up until the end of the seventeenth century, the word for fox was *goupil*. The animal in the fable was a *goupil* named Renart – a form of the Germanic name Reinhard. Renart was so popular that the French word for fox was actually changed from *goupil* to *renard* because of him!

Chantecler the Rooster

Now, what about that rooster? Ever since those medieval French people heard the story of Renart and the rooster called Chantecler, they have been giving the same name to their own roosters. Chantecler comes from two French words: *chanter* (to sing) and *cler* or *clair* (loudly or clearly). So, it's easy to see why it's a fitting rooster name. Even so, nobody felt the need to change the existing word for rooster – which is still *coq*.

The Fable of Renart and Chantecler

This is a brief summary of the fable of Renart and Chantecler:

Chantecler lived on a farm with his harem of hens. Their enclosure had a thick hedge around it to keep them all safe. But one day, Renart the fox managed to climb over it and get into the chicken yard. The fox approached Chantecler who was wary of him at first. But Renart was a smooth-talking fox, and he finally convinced the rooster that he was just a fan of crowing. He wanted to hear Chantecler crow and see if he could crow as loudly as his father had.

After a bit of banter, Chantecler was convinced that the fox was harmless, and he wanted to crow about his crowing. The rooster closed his eyes and stuck out his neck to let out his loudest crow ever. As he did, the fox grabbed him by the neck, jumped over the hedge, and headed for the woods with poor Chantecler in his mouth.

The hens squawked out the alarm, and the farmhands and the dog chased after the fox. They were yelling at him and calling him all sorts of names. This gave Chantecler an idea. Even though the fox had him by the throat, the rooster was somehow still able to talk. He said, "I can't believe you're running like a coward. Can't you hear all the names those peasants are calling you? You should turn around and insult them too."

This sounded like a good idea to Renart, so he turned around to do just that. But as soon as he opened his mouth to shout at the farmhands, Chantecler made a break for it and flew up into a tree.

It seems that the fox and the rooster both learned a lesson that day: Renart learned that sometimes it's better to keep your mouth closed, and Chantecler learned that sometimes you have to keep your eyes open. Of course, there is a bit more to the fable than that, but this was the little tale that changed *goupils* into *renards* and caused everyone to start naming their roosters Chantecler.

The stories from *Le Roman de Renart* (The Book of Renart) were recounted throughout medieval Europe from about the twelfth century. Then, in the fourteenth century, Geoffrey Chaucer adapted the story of Renart and Chantecler as part of the Nun's Priest's Tale in the *Canterbury Tales*. This helped to popularize it in England where the characters were known as Reynard and Chanticleer.

Another Famous Chantecler

In the early 1900s another Chantecler stuck out his neck and began to crow. Edmond Rostand (author of *Cyrano de Bergerac*) wrote a fable-based play with a rooster as the star of the show. And, of course, the obvious name for that rooster was Chantecler.

In this play, the very cocky Chantecler believed that it was his crowing that caused the sun to rise every morning. Then one day he fell in love with a beautiful pheasant hen who had flown into the barnyard to escape a hunter. Chantecler's thoughts were only for her, and one morning he forgot to crow. He became a laughing-stock among the other animals when the sun rose without his help. But don't worry, Chantecler did redeem himself when he fought off a hawk who was trying to pick up the ingredients for a chicken dinner. This play deepened even more the association of roosters with the name Chantecler.

Since the Gallic rooster (*coq*) is a symbol of France, there are rooster images everywhere, and the term "Chantecler" is often mentioned. These days Chantecler is also a popular name for restaurants, hotels, companies, etc. (For example, the Michelin-starred restaurant at the Negresco Hotel in Nice, France is called Chantecler.)

So there you have the tale of Renart, the former *goupil*, and Chantecler, the cocky *coq*. Now whenever you see or hear a reference to them, you'll know the whole story.

∾

Note on Spelling:

Old French: Renart and Chantecler

Modern French: Renard and Chantecler

English: Reynard and Chanticleer

Cocorico! Cocorico!
Now the sun can rise!

FRENCH FROGGIES

*H*ave you ever wondered why the French are sometimes referred to as frogs? As with many traditions that go back hundreds or thousands of years, the origin is unclear. However, there are several theories about how this most unusual moniker came to be associated with our friends in France...

Frog Legs

The first theory is that the French are called frogs because they eat frog legs – *cuisses de grenouilles*. But the French weren't the first or only people to eat frogs. In fact an archaeology site in the UK that dates back to the sixth century BC found evidence of cooked frogs in England.

However, the first known mention of eating frogs in "modern" Europe is indeed found in France: to be exact, in the records of the French Catholic Church to be exact.

It was the twelfth century and the church leaders noticed that the monks were getting a bit too pudgy. They tried to help them stay slim by ordering them not to eat meat on certain days. So, the crafty, meat-loving monks had frogs declared as fish. They could eat something meaty, obey church laws, and still fill out their extra-large robes.

The hungry peasants, who had no trouble watching their weight, immediately recognized frogs as a free source of nutrition... And the French have been eating frogs ever since.

King Clovis and Frogs

Another possible source for the froggy nickname is the banner of Clovis I. Clovis, who is known as the first Christian king of France, had three black toads on his flag. This symbol had been handed down by his father by the other Merovingian kings before him. Clovis was crowned in 481, aged 15. Like his father, he was a pagan, but his wife Clotilde was urging him to become a Catholic Christian.

The story goes that after one of his victorious battles, an angel came to him and told him to change his emblem from toads to fleurs de lys (we'll talk more about those in the next chapter). He converted to Catholicism in 496 and was baptized in Reims on Christmas Day in 508. This set the stage for all of France to become a Catholic nation, a connection which lasted until the French Revolution.

In the seventeenth century, the fact that frogs had been the symbol of the Merovingian kings was common knowledge. In 1659 when the French took Arras, a city in the north of

France which had been under Spanish rule, people claimed that it was one of Nostradamus' prophecies coming true.

Nostradamus had said: *Les anciens crapauds prendront Sara*, meaning "the ancient toads shall take Sara." They reasoned that Sara was "Aras" spelled backwards, and the ancient toads referred to the French and the old symbol of the three toads.

Frogs Live in Swamps

Another theory on the frog nickname has to do with Parisian swamps. The right bank of the Seine River in Paris used to be a big old swamp. A reminder of that is in the name of the now trendy area called the Marais. Marais means swamp or marshland. Even though the stagnant water dried up around the ninth century, the area's soggy reputation hung around for hundreds of years.

It seems that those living the high life at the court at Versailles referred to the people of Paris as frogs because they lived in the former swampland. In the *Dictionary of Phrase and Fable* of 1898 compiled by E. Cobham Brewer, we find the phrase *Qu'en disent les grenouilles?* - "What do the frogs (people of Paris) say?"

The French association with frogs was so deep in the British mind that they used it as a general name for a Frenchman: They called him Monsieur Jean Crapaud (Mr. John Toad). It was also written as Johnny Crappeau and Johnny Crappo. This was a national personification much like John Bull for an Englishman.

Toads and Frogs

A *crapaud* is a toad, and a *grenouille* is a frog. The amphibians on Clovis' flag were toads, but over the years the French toads morphed into frogs. In addition, the words "French" and "frog" both start with "fr" so French froggies just sounds better than French toads.

ENGLISH ROAST BEEF

The British have been calling the French frogs for hundreds of years, but the name-calling goes both ways. Those French froggies have a nice little nickname for the British too: They call them *Rosbifs*.

Rosbif is the Frenchification of "roast beef." Yes, that big chunk of beef served up for Sunday dinner. It seems that this strange nickname has several possible explanations as well.

First of all, there is the obvious reference to the food called roast beef. This method of cooking where the outside of the meat is well done and the inside is still red was an English invention. At the time the French were still boiling their beef and found this British culinary invention quite tasty. The English people became associated with this popular British food.

Another theory was that the red uniforms of the British reminded the French of the color of rare roast beef.

And the third reference is to pasty, white British skin. Since many Brits have very light skin they don't do well in the sun. After a few hours on the beach, some British people do turn red like roast beef. (And, I'm afraid I'm one of them.)

Name-calling

Please note that calling the French frogs and the British *rosbifs* is mildly derogatory, but can sometimes be used in good-natured teasing. Name-calling aside, there are some interesting historical facts to be learned from these nicknames.

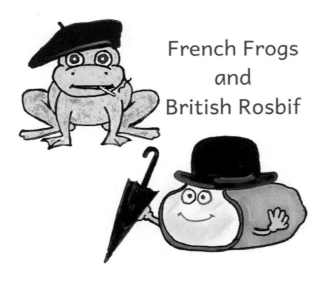

French Frogs
and
British Rosbif

FLEUR DE LYS

THE IRIS OF KINGS

*GW*e have just read about how King Clovis was divinely inspired to change the images on his coat of arms from toads to fleurs de lys, so let's find out a bit more about this interesting symbol...

The fleur de lys is a stylized flower that has a long association with the kings of France. There are two spellings for this floral emblem – *fleur de lis* and *fleur de lys*. Both can be used to refer to the botanical lily flower or the symbol.

Fleur de lys literally means "flower of the lily." This might lead you to think that the symbol represents a stylized lily. The only problem is that it doesn't look like a lily flower... And that's because it's not. It's really an iris, and specifically a yellow iris that grows at the water's edge.

So why call an iris a lily? The confusion seems to lie with the word *lys* or *lis*. There's a river that runs from Pas de

Calais in northern France to Ghent, Belgium. This river is called the Leie or Lys. And it has lots of yellow iris along its banks. Since the early Frankish kings were from that area, it seems likely that the fleur de lys represents the flower that grows on the Lys River. The fleurs de lys on the old French flags are gold (like the yellow iris) and the background is blue (like the Lys River).

The first historical evidence we have of the fleur de lys on the shield or coat of arms of the French kings dates to the twelfth century and Louis VI. His blue shield was strewn with golden fleurs de lys. This scattering of the symbols was used until the late fourteenth century when Charles V changed it to a group of three. It's also in the twelfth century that we begin to find writings explaining the fifth-century origin of the link between the fleur de lys symbol and the French kings.

Clovis and his Iris

One story links the fleur de lys with King Clovis' conversion to Christianity. Clovis was facing a battle with a much stronger army. But he wasn't worried because he had faith in his ancestral shield. Then just before the battle began, the symbols on his shield changed to golden fleurs de lys on a blue background. Clovis threw it down and quickly grabbed a new shield. The same thing happened three times, and Clovis was running out of time (and shields). He had to go into battle with the fleurs de lys. He fought fiercely and was victorious.

Confused but happy, the King told his wife about the golden flowers appearing on his shield. The Queen assured him that God had helped him win the battle. She said the three flowers represented the holy trinity and would bring him a long life. The gold color meant he would reign over a golden age, and the blue background represented the heaven that he was promised if he believed in the true God. That was enough to convince Clovis and he became a Christian like his wife. He kept the fleur de lys as his symbol.

Another legend tells us that Clovis and his army were in battle and were pushed back into the marsh lands. They were trapped and would surely have been slaughtered had they not spotted a group of yellow water iris. Knowing that these flowers grew in shallow water, Clovis saw where his troops could safely cross the waters and escape. According to this legend, this is the reason Clovis adopted the yellow flower as his symbol.

In some stories, an angel comes down from heaven with a holy flask shaped like a fleur de lys and pours out holy oil to anoint Clovis. These legends, which surfaced around the twelfth century, might have been invented to indicate Louis VI's divine right to rule and to link him to the early Frankish kings. Of course, that doesn't mean that King Clovis didn't really use the fleur de lys on his shield. We just haven't come across any proof of it yet.

Even though the fleur de lys has a strong association with French royalty, it has also been used by other countries, cities, and organizations through the years.

Note on Spelling:

Fleur de lys - singular
Fleurs de lys - plural

Fleurs de lys growing along the riverbank

TRICOLOUR FLAG

FROM FLOWERS TO STRIPES

*I*t was during the Revolution that the three-colored French flag of today was adopted. Before that, the monarchy's flag (which featured the fleur de lys) was also the national flag.

The story of the striped French flag started with a cockade. At the beginning of the Revolution, people wore cockades (round rosettes of fabric) on their hats. The color of a person's cockade indicated their political leanings. The Paris militia wore cockades of red and blue, which were the colors of Paris: Blue was for Saint Martin and red was for Saint Denis.

General Lafayette thought white should be added. He said it was the ancient color of France, but others saw it as the color of the monarchy. Whatever the origin of the white, it was added between the blue and red. And the tricolour cockade was born. It was adopted as part of the uniform of the National Guard and became a very important symbol of the Revolution.

The French people grew fond of their red, white, and blue cockades, and these fabric rosettes were the inspiration for the new French flag. The new three-color flag was adopted in 1790, but the original version was red, white, and blue, with red being nearest the flagpole. In 1794 it was redesigned and the colors were shuffled into the order we know today: blue, white, and red, with the blue nearest the pole.

The French flag is affectionately called the *bleu, blanc, rouge* (blue, white, red) or the *tricolore* (tricolour). Sometimes the three colors are seen as representing the three-word motto of France: *liberté, égalité, fraternité* (liberty, equality, fraternity) which was also popularized during the Revolution.

Today, the three bands of color on the French flag are of equal width, but originally, the stripes got slightly wider the farther away they were from the pole: The blue was 30%, white was 33%, and red 37%. This was because when the flag was waving in the breeze the outer bands would appear smaller. But under Napoleon I, the design was revised to make them all nice and equal.

Even though the flag was designed and adopted during the Revolution, it was rarely flown then. It was Napoleon who really put it into use. But in 1814 when Napoleon was ousted, his three-colored flag went with him. The monarchy was restored and the new Bourbon King, Louis XVIII, declared his white flag with its three fleurs de lys as the national flag. That monarchy and its flag lasted from 1814 until 1830. Then the French had another revolution (the July Revolution) and the fleur de lys flag was thrown out along with the king.

During the tumultuous days of the 1830 July Revolution, Charles X resigned and Louis Philippe was installed as King. The new king was known as the "citizen king." Louis Philippe had supported the Revolution in 1789, but had fled into exile to escape the Reign of Terror. He brought back the Revolutionary, tricolour flag that he knew the people loved.

The blue, white, and red flag has been in use since then, but it was almost replaced in 1870. The Second Empire had ended and the second Napoleon had been deposed. At this point, the royalists were in the majority in the National Assembly, and they wanted to reestablish the monarchy.

They asked Henri, Count of Chambord, the last legitimate male heir of Louis XV, to come and be their new king. He was giving it some thought, and for a while it looked like the monarchy would be back in business. But there was one little glitch. Henri didn't like the new striped flag. He said he would only consent to be king if they brought back the white flag with the fleurs de lys on it. If he was to be king, he didn't want any reminders of Revolutions Past.

Well, that was a deal-breaker. The French loved their new revolution-inspired, tricolour flag. The National Assembly suggested that the king could have the fleur de lys on his own personal flag, and the nation would keep their *bleu, blanc, rouge* that they liked so much. Henri said, "No deal!" It was fleur de lys for the nation or nothing at all.

So it seems that the French monarchy was toppled by the Revolution, but it kept popping back up until it was done away with one and for all by its own symbol, the fleur de lys.

92

PART V: TAKING TO THE STREETS

REVOLUTIONS TO DEMONSTRATIONS

*T*he Revolution is an important part of French history. It shaped French ideas and identity in ways that endure to this day.

This section starts out with Marianne, the personification of the French Republic. She'll tell us, in her own words, how she has changed throughout France's history. We go on to talk about the infamous guillotine, the French national anthem, and how the French people show their displeasure with the government today.

MARIANNE

THE CHANGING FACE OF THE FRENCH REPUBLIC

fter the French deposed their king during the Revolution of 1789, they had a difficult time settling into a new form of government. During the 81 years that followed that first revolution, they had two failed republics, three more kings, two emperors, and two more revolutions before the third try at a republic took hold in 1870.

Of course, that wasn't the last republic as France is now in its fifth one, but the country has remained a republic since then, except for a short time during the German occupation of World War II.

At the beginning of the first revolution, Marianne became a personification of the French Republic, and her transformation follows the history of France. But I think I'll let her tell you about it in her own words...

Marianne's Story

Did you know that France has been led by a woman ever since the French Revolution of 1789? It's true! My name is Marianne and my image is on official seals and postage stamps. Sculpted busts of me adorn city halls and public buildings throughout the country. Every French person can easily recognize me, but no one can describe exactly what I look like. That's because I have regular makeovers. After all, I'm the personification of the French Republic, so I have to keep up with the times and always look my best.

Before I became the symbol of the Republic, though, I was the goddess of Liberty. I wore Roman clothing and held a red Phrygian cap on top of a spear. The Phrygian cap used to be worn in ancient Rome by freed slaves to show their liberated status so it was an important symbol.

Marianne as the Goddess of Liberty holding her Phrygian bonnet on a spike

When the Revolution began in 1789, the French people looked to me to inspire them in their struggle for liberty. Later, the Revolutionaries adopted my red cap and it became a symbol of their Revolution.

FIRST REPUBLIC 1792-1804

From Warrior to Mother

After the old order was overthrown, France needed a new form of government and the First French Republic was formed in 1792. Since there was no longer a king, this new government needed a symbol to replace his image on their official seal. They decided to employ me, the goddess of Liberty, to represent their new Republic. Of course, I was flattered and I accepted immediately.

On the new State seal, I stood in my traditional pose, wearing Roman attire and holding a red Phrygian cap of liberty atop a spike. On my left, there was a bundle of sticks with an axe attached. This is called a "fasces" and it's another emblem from Roman times. It was carried by the magistrate's body guard and symbolized his power to carry out punishment, either by beating (with the sticks) or by beheading (with the axe). Unfortunately, this would be an all too relevant symbol for the bloody times to come.

Every image of the king was replaced by an image of me – the new face of France. And under my picture were the words, "French Republic." Soon, the people started to call me Marianne. I think it was because Marie, Anne, and Marie-Anne were the most popular names among the common people at that time. I took that name proudly and it made me feel like one of them.

The First Republic got off to a very rocky start and was, almost immediately, thrown into that horrible Reign of Terror. Because of political disagreements, an estimated 40,000 of my precious people were executed. Many went by way of the guillotine which, I'm ashamed to say, came to be called the "national razor" of France. Those were terrible days!

Finally, people grew tired of the bloodshed. They needed a change and so did I. It was time for a makeover. I transformed my image from the axe-wielding lady on the seal into a serene motherly figure. I hoped that it would calm and soothe my "children." On the 1793 calendar, I began *wearing* my Phrygian liberty cap. The spear that used to hold it was gone, as were all weapons. I calmly read a book surrounded by symbols of knowledge. I became the model of a serene Republic longing for liberty, peace, and enlightenment.

As a peaceful mother figure calmly reading a
book. The spike and all other weapons are
gone and she is wearing her Phrygian cap.

ONE EMPEROR, THREE KINGS, AND TWO MORE REVOLUTIONS 1804-1848

Woman of the People

That First Republic lasted only 12 years. It came to an end in 1804, when Napoleon Bonaparte became emperor. Since there was no longer a republic, I was no longer needed as its symbol. So, I went back to being simply a representation of Liberty. It's a status that I maintained for the next 44 years while France went through one emperor, three kings, and two more revolutions.

Even though I no longer had a republic to represent, I didn't abandon the French people and they didn't forget about me either. Eugène Delacroix featured me in a very well-known painting called, *La Liberté guidant le peuple*. In English that's "Liberty leading the people." I had changed my looks again. He painted me as a barefoot, bare-breasted woman – I'm not quite sure why, but that one sleeve always seems to fall down. Anyway, I'm holding the French flag and leading a group of fighters during the 1830 revolution. I had left my Roman goddess image behind to become a woman of the people, willing to fight alongside them for liberty.

SECOND REPUBLIC 1848-1852

Which Look for Me?

After the third Revolution in 1848, the French gave the Republic another try and Republic No. 2 was formed. The new government declared that *"the image of liberty should replace everywhere the images of corruption and shame..."* My status as symbol of the State was restored, and now I represented Liberty, the Republic, and the Revolution. As the official symbol of the government, my image would grace statues, money, important documents, etc. However, the *powers that were* just weren't sure how they wanted me to look.

They held a contest to get ideas from different artists. They wanted me to portray the motto "liberty, equality, and fraternity." Many lovely illustrations were submitted and I couldn't decide which one I liked best. Neither could the government. They had intended to choose one look and standardize my image throughout the country, but since the Second Republic only lasted four years, my makeover project was left unfinished.

THE SECOND EMPIRE

Booted Out Again

You would think the French people would have known better. But no, Louis-Napoleon Bonaparte (Napoleon III) was elected president of the Second Republic. And when it was time for new elections he, like his uncle before him, decided to declare himself emperor. So the Republic fell by the wayside – again, and I lost my status as its symbol – again.

Marianne: any daughter of France

THIRD REPUBLIC 1870-1940

Which Hat to Wear?

When Napoleon III was captured by the Prussians in 1870, the Third Republic was formed and I was back – this time for good. Busts of me were sculpted and placed all over France to replace those of the former emperor. Republic No. 3 wanted to avoid all symbols of revolt, so they preferred that I wear a crown of leaves or sun rays instead of my Phrygian cap which was now associated with revolution.

However, I liked my red cap and so did the people. In 1880 the Paris city hall ordered a bust of me wearing my Phrygian bonnet. Soon other cities followed, and I was again free to wear the head covering that I had grown so fond of. It was, after all, a symbol of liberty, an ideal very close to all our hearts. The cap-wearing version of me became the most popular one, and today, you'll see me wearing my liberty bonnet in town halls, schools, and public buildings all across France.

Sadly, the Third Republic ended in 1940 with the German Occupation. I was again officially retired from public life, but I lived on in the hearts of the French people as their symbol of Liberty.

FOURTH AND FIFTH REPUBLICS 1946-PRESENT

A Woman of Many Looks

The Fourth and Fifth Republics followed the liberation of France and the busts of me came out of attics and closets. They reclaimed their rightful places of honor in town halls and public buildings.

There has never been an official image of me, so artists are free to imagine me as they wish. Likewise, mayors are free to choose the version that suits them to grace their town halls. Historically, the women who posed for paintings or sculptures of me were anonymous; I could have been any daughter of the Republic. But in the 1960s, someone had the idea to sculpt me in the likeness of famous actresses and singers. The first one to pose in my place was Brigitte Bardot in 1968. She was followed by Michèle Morgan, Mireille Mathieu, Catherine Deneuve, Inès de la Fressange, Laetitia Casta, and Sophie Marceau. I certainly can't complain about being represented by these lovely ladies!

Through all their struggles and revolutions I've never left the side of my beloved French people. I've changed my image from goddess to anonymous woman of the people to famous actress. I've taken on the role of fearless warrior, comforting mother and, as long as they'll have me, I intend to do my best to become whatever the French people need me to be in the future. After all, it does a girl good to have a makeover from time to time.

THE GUILLOTINE

DR. GUILLOTIN AND HIS GUILLOTINE

*D*r. Joseph Ignace Guillotin's name will forever be
linked to the infamous head-severing machine of
the French Revolution, the *guillotine*. But why? He neither
invented nor designed the so-called, "national razor." He
was, however, a politically active doctor who lobbied for
equal and humane treatment of the condemned. But one
day, while addressing the National Assembly, he got a bit
over-enthusiastic about his subject...

At the end of 1789, Dr. Guillotin was delivering a
passionate speech to the newly established government
about how the ideals of the Revolution should apply to the
death penalty. The Revolution was about equality. If all men
were to be treated equally, then why should the methods of
execution be different?

Why should nobles be decapitated by saber, which was
considered more humane because it usually took only one
pass, while commoners went by way of the hatchet, which

might take multiple attempts and cause more suffering? Enemies of the state were quartered, heretics were burned at the stake, thieves were put on the wheel or hung, and counterfeiters were boiled alive. Guillotin argued that killing someone was punishment enough, and that it wasn't necessary to torture them as well.

After pointing out the problems with the current system, he presented his answer – a machine. He was convinced that a well-designed machine would deliver swift, reliable, equitable, and practically painless justice for all.

He also had the radical idea that public executions should *not* be seen as entertainment. He hoped that speedy executions would be boring enough to make the jeering crowds lose interest.

A Little Slip of the Tongue

But in Dr. G's excitement about his revolutionary idea, he got a bit carried away and a little too personal. He boasted to the Assembly, "With *my* machine, I will cut off *your* head in the blink of an eye and *you* won't suffer at all." This sent a wave of laughter through the audience, and since he had called it *his* machine, they immediately named it "Guillotin's guillotine." (Since the word "machine" is feminine in French, they added an "e" to Guillotin's name to make it feminine.)

Before this speech, the machine had been nicknamed the "louison," or "louisette," after Dr. Antoine Louis who had drawn up the preliminary design. It was eventually built by Schmidt, a German mechanic living in Paris ... But neither the designer nor the builder of the machine got the "honor" of attaching their name to their invention. The name "guillotine" stuck.

The good doctor protested. He didn't want a machine of death named after him – but it was too late. Newspaper articles, songs and poems were written about the "guillotine," and the device was forever linked to the unfortunate doctor's name.

Who Will Build It?

In 1791, after a year and a half of lobbying by Dr. Guillotin, torture was legally banned and beheading by guillotine was proclaimed the only method to be used for capital punishment.

There was one little problem, however. The Assembly forgot to form a committee to actually build it. So criminals were being condemned to death who, by law, had to be beheaded by machine. But there was no machine to do the job. People were getting anxious as the prisons filled with criminals and there were no executions/entertainment in the public squares.

When the Assembly recognized their little oversight, Dr. Antoine Louis, the medical expert at the Academy of Surgery who had drawn the initial plans, was put in charge. He consulted with Schmidt, a German mechanic, who made adjustments and built the machine.

King Louis and the Blade

According to the *Memoires de Sanson*, a book written by the royal executioner, the King also had some input on the design of the guillotine. Louis XVI was still king at the beginning of the Revolution, even though his powers had been limited. As a lover of all things mechanical, he was keen to see the design for this revolutionary new machine. After viewing the preliminary sketches with Dr. Guillotin, Dr. Louis, and Sanson (the executioner), King Louis was pleased with the idea, but had a suggestion to make. The committee had envisioned a convex blade, but the King pointed out that a slanted blade would sever the vertebrae more easily. It was agreed and the King picked up a pen and changed the design. (A few years later when Louis XVI was lying with his head in the guillotine waiting for the blade to drop, he was probably hoping that he had been right about that blade.)

Execution as Entertainment

The guillotine made its public debut in April 1792. A big crowd turned out to see the new and much talked-about machine. What a letdown. The spectators booed the executioner and grumbled among themselves. It was too fast – just a few seconds and it was over. It was hardly worth making the trip to the public square. They wanted to bring back the longer-lasting hangings.

In the early days, the guillotine would be assembled in the square when needed and taken down after the executions. But the new beheading machine began to see so much action, that four months later, it was left in place permanently. Only the blade was removed after each execution (or group of executions).

As the Revolution became more violent and turned into the Reign of Terror, "enemies of the Revolution" were losing their heads on a wholesale scale. People could be brought to trial for any suspected infraction and find themselves headless within hours. More guillotines were needed to keep up with demand and it was decreed that there should be at least one guillotine in each of the French departments.

Even though the crowds had been disappointed that the guillotine did its job so quickly, soon there were enough people being beheaded that the "show" got longer and more interesting. The guillotine became the symbol of the Revolution and was adopted as part of French culture.

People were desensitized to beheadings and even developed a certain fondness for Guillotin's machine. Some of the nicknames given to it were: National Razor, Windmill of Silence, The Widow, Capet's Tie (after the death of King Louis XVI, whose name was Louis Capet), and Madame la Guillotine. Being beheaded was called "sneezing in the sack" – a reference to the bag at the foot of the guillotine to catch the falling heads.

At executions, programs were distributed listing the "beheadings of the day" and their crimes. Women adorned themselves with jewelry in the shape of "Capet's tie" while their children played with their toy "national razors." On the dinner table, miniature guillotines sliced the family's fruit and desserts.

Would you like them both sliced, Madame?

Dr. Guillotin's Head

Sometimes it's incorrectly reported that the guillotine claimed the head of its namesake. But this confusion came about when a Dr. J.M.V. Guillotin from Lyon was beheaded. Our Dr. Joseph Ignace Guillotin, of guillotine fame, died with his head intact. He did have a close call though. He was imprisoned and might have lost his head, but Robespierre (who was leading the Reign of Terror) came into contact with the national razor first, and Dr. Guillotin was released from prison. Phew! That was a close call!

While Dr. Guillotin was glad his head was still attached, he regretted that his name was linked to the machine that had severed so many others. Later, he would call it the "involuntary stain on his life." Victor Hugo seemed to understand

Doctor G's pain when he said, "Some men are unhappy: Christopher Columbus, because he couldn't give his name to his discovery, and Guillotin, because he couldn't separate his name from his invention."

Poor Dr. Guillotin had tried to do something good for humanity, but through a few ill-chosen words, he had associated his name with one of the most horrific episodes in French history... I guess that just goes to show that you should always choose your words carefully, and never lose your head.

～

SOME INTERESTING GUILLOTINE FACTS:

- The guillotine was used in France from 1792 until 1977. The last public execution by guillotine was in 1939, after which they were private. The last time the guillotine dropped in France was in 1977, and the State abolished the death penalty in 1981.
- Even today in France, some tools used for slicing are known as guillotines. There is a *guillotine à saussison* (sausage slicer), *guillotine à fromage* (cheese slicer), *guillotine à pain* (bread slicer), *guillotine à foie gras* (foie gras slicer), and a *guillotine à papier* (paper cutter).
- The French didn't invent beheading machines. Similar machines have been used at different times and in different countries since the Middle Ages.

But the French made theirs a symbol of their Revolution and now when anyone thinks of the guillotine, they think of France.

- The German mechanic, Schmidt, tweaked the design of Dr. Louis. Instead of pulling a cord, the executioner only pushed a button. Schmidt decided to patent his invention. But when the minister of the interior read the application, he responded, "It is repugnant to humanity to give a patent for a discovery of this type. We have not yet reached that level of barbarism."

- The guillotine was either painted red or built with a wood that was naturally red (for obvious reasons).

- Hitler ordered 20 guillotines from France in 1936 and used them to kill 16,500 people during the Holocaust.

- If you want to see a guillotine, there is one in London at Madame Tussauds wax museum.

THE MARSEILLAISE

A REVOLUTIONARY ANTHEM

France's rousing national anthem, the Marseillaise, was written during the French Revolution. In 1792 the Revolution was in full swing, and all the monarchies of Europe were nervous. It made them uneasy to see people rise up against a king. It was in their best interest to put a stop to all that revolutionary ruckus lest their own subjects decide to do away with them too.

Austria, Marie Antoinette's homeland, was threatening to invade France. So, France beat them to the punch and declared war on them. On 25 April 1792, news of the declaration of war reached Strasbourg. The mayor held a banquet for the troops stationed there who would soon be marching off to fight. Patriotic fervor filled the room as the soldiers and officers celebrated the victories they were sure would be theirs.

Claude Joseph Rouget de Lisle

Among the banqueting soldiers was Captain Rouget de Lisle, a 32-year-old military engineer from eastern France. The mayor knew that Rouget de Lisle wrote songs and poems, so he asked him to write a song that would stir the hearts of the soldiers and inspire them as they went into battle.

He thought the French Revolution needed a more rousing anthem than the current one. They had been revolting to a song called *Ça ira, ça ira* (It Will Be Fine, It Will Be Fine). This barely optimistic song title had been inspired by Benjamin Franklin when he was ambassador to France during the American Revolution. Whenever anyone asked Ben about the progress of the American War of Independence he would answer, "*Ça ira, ça ira.*"

So, Rouget de Lisle was given a formidable task. He should write a song that would stir up patriotism and enthusiasm in the hearts of the soldiers and the people of France and lead their nation into victory. That's all. And it would be really great if he could do it that very night.

Words and Music

It was quite a responsibility, and Rouget de Lisle must have left the party murmuring, "Oh la la! 'ow eez it possible? 'ow will I find ze words? And ze music?" His head was spinning as he started for home – then he noticed a poster on the side of a building, which said "Take up your arms, citizens! Form your battalions!"

"Hmm," Rouget de Lisle thought, "That's not bad. Maybe I can use that in my song." He grabbed his notebook and pencil and jotted it down. As he walked on, he saw more posters and they all had patriotic slogans on them. He went all over town looking for posters and copying down their messages. Many of those poster slogans ended up in the song lyrics he wrote that night.

As for the music... well, he was probably inspired by other tunes that he had heard. There are several claims that the French national anthem sounds a lot like other songs, but there weren't any copyright laws in those days and borrowing tunes was an accepted practice. After all, the

American anthem borrowed music from a British pub tune, and the British anthem may have been written for a French king.

At the end of the day, the important thing is that by morning, Captain Rouget de Lisle had put together a stirring song. Its original title was *Chant de Guerre pour l'Armée du Rhin* (War Song for the Rhine Army). It was a rousing tune and the mayor himself sang it the following evening when it was presented to the officers.

Why is It Called the Marseillaise?

The song was written in Strasbourg, but the soldiers there might not have had sufficient time to learn it before marching off into battle. However, a few months later, down in Marseille in the south of France, a singer performed Rouget de Lisle's song. It aroused such patriotism that the National Guard of Marseille adopted it as their marching song.

When a group of volunteers from Marseille set out for Paris, they marched to this song all through France. It stirred everyone who heard it, and all along the way men were moved to join the army. When the Marseille troops arrived in Paris they were still singing "War Song for the Rhine Army" at the top of their lungs. Since that title was way too long, the song became known as La Marseillaise after the troops that brought it to Paris.

National Anthem

The French National Convention adopted it as the New Republic's anthem on 14 July 1795. But when Napoleon became emperor in 1804, he did away with it – he didn't want to encourage any revolution where he might end up like the former King.

Then, the Third Republic came along, and in 1879 the Marseillaise was reinstated as the French national anthem. Throughout the years there has been a lot of controversy around the song. It was, after all, a song written to spur on a revolution so some of the words can be a bit violent. But it has stood the test of time and will probably be around for quite a while yet.

If you would like to sing along with the French, here are the words in French and English:

French

> *Allons enfants de la Patrie,*
> *Le jour de gloire est arrivé!*
> *Contre nous de la tyrannie,*
> *L'étendard sanglant est levé, (bis)*
> *Entendez-vous dans les campagnes*
> *Mugir ces féroces soldats?*
> *Ils viennent jusque dans vos bras*
> *Égorger vos fils, vos compagnes!*

> *Aux armes, citoyens,*
> *Formez vos bataillons,*
> *Marchons, marchons!*
> *Qu'un sang impur*
> *Abreuve nos sillons!*

English

Arise, children of the Fatherland,
The day of glory has arrived!
Against us, tyranny's
Bloody standard is raised, (repeat)
Do you hear, in the countryside,
The roar of those ferocious soldiers?
They're coming right into your arms
To cut the throats of your sons, your women!

    To arms, citizens,
    Form your battalions,
    Let's march, let's march!
    Let an impure blood
    Water our furrows!

DEMONSTRATIONS, STRIKES, AND BOSSNAPPINGS

When the French are unhappy about something, they don't keep quiet – they draw attention to their cause. And there are three main ways they do this: Demonstrations, Strikes, and (if things get really desperate) Bossnappings...

DEMONSTRATIONS – MANIFESTATIONS

The French love to march in the streets. If they have a grievance, they get together, make signs, and demonstrate. They even join marches that have nothing to do with them or their situation. They just support everyone's right to protest (and maybe they like parades).

These demonstrations are known as *manifestations* in France, and they are definitely part of the culture. They are often about social issues, anti-war, anti-racism, etc. - but they can also be for workers' rights or to show displeasure with the government.

The most well-known of these manifestations started the French Revolution back in 1789. When the people were fed up with their government, they took to the streets to make their unhappiness known – and they certainly did! They overthrew the king and formed a Republic.

Their new government was founded on the ideas of the Enlightenment movement and the belief that the only legitimate power lies with the people. So when the people aren't happy with their elected officials and they take to the streets, the government pays attention. There is always someone there to take an official headcount so those in power will know exactly how popular these views are. (They don't want another revolution on their hands.)

With all these unhappy people marching in the streets, things can sometimes get out of hand. Throughout France's history there have been many violent demonstrations. Up until the 1920s, deaths during protests were not uncommon and the army was often called in to bring order. Thankfully, today's manifestations are usually more peaceful events.

STRIKES – GRÈVES

To be on strike is called *être en grève* in French. This expression comes from the Place de Grève (now Place de l'Hôtel de Ville) in Paris along the River Seine. The word *grève* referred to a sandy area where cargo boats would pull in. It was where unemployed men would gather to get work loading or unloading the boats.

At that time, *être en grève* meant to be without work. The meaning of the expression changed around the first part of the nineteenth century when workers who felt that their bosses were taking advantage of them decided to stop working. They basically made themselves unemployed (*en*

119

grève), and instead of going to work, they gathered at the Place de Grève.

Today the French still go on strike (a lot) to call attention to their rights as workers. But, being French, they go about it a bit differently than some other countries. In the UK and the US, for example, if there is a conflict between workers and management, talks are held to see if the problems can be resolved. Then, if there is no satisfaction, there might be a strike.

But not in France. The French take action first and talk later. They strike and disrupt services to draw attention to their situation. If they can cause enough problems, talks begin.

BOSSNAPPING – LA SÉQUESTRATION DE PATRON

Bossnapping is a very strange phenomenon (at least to the non-French). The first time I heard about this, I couldn't believe my ears – I thought it was a problem with my understanding of the French language. But it wasn't.

Bossnapping is when disgruntled workers barricade their bosses in their offices and hold them hostage until there is a resolution between labor and management – or at least until talks are underway.

The bosses are normally treated well: They are given food and drink and not abused in any way. And as long as that's the case, the police usually don't intervene. Most of these situations have been resolved peacefully.

Bossnapping has been practiced in France at least since 1968, but really came to worldwide attention in 2009 when a wave of bossnappings swept the country. Bosses were advised to keep a little survival kit in their office when there was the threat of unrest.

In the wake of all these bossnappings, then president, Nicolas Sarkozy, denounced the practice. He bravely declared that even disgruntled workers must obey the law – and holding people hostage was, indeed, against the law. However, a public opinion poll, taken at the time, showed that the public was still sympathetic toward the workers.

But times are changing in France and the French are turning away from kidnapping their bosses. In 2016, eight workers from Goodyear tire factory in France were given nine-month jail sentences for a bossnapping that took place two years earlier. So, it seems that bossnapping may be a thing of the past in France, we'll just have to wait and see.

PART VI: ARCHITECTURE AND RELATED STORIES

GARGOYLES TO FARTERS

The last part of this book concerns architecture (or at least stories related to buildings). We start with a legend explaining why Gothic churches, like Notre Dame, are decorated with gargoyles. Then we move on to curious histories connected to the Eiffel Tower and the Moulin Rouge.

GARGOYLES

A SAINT, A CONVICT, AND A GARGOYLE GO INTO A SWAMP

On a trip through northern France, I was intrigued by all the gargoyles on the Gothic churches and wondered why these mythical creatures were chosen to adorn houses of God. Then I came across this legend which seems like a pretty reasonable explanation to me.

This story takes place in the seventh century. It has been retold many times over the last 1400 years resulting in several adaptations. This is my version. Enjoy!

TROUBLE IN THE SWAMP

It all started in misty and mysterious ancient times. In Normandy, France where the Seine River snakes through the land, a town now known as Rouen was having a crisis.

A fearsome monster had taken up residence in the marshes along the banks of the river. While he looked like your normal, garden-variety serpent/dragon, he was a bit different. Instead of breathing fire out his mouth like most dragons, he belched out floods of water.

He was causing havoc along the river: sinking ships and eating the passengers, flooding fields and eating the people and animals that he drowned. Basically, he was eating anyone and anything that crossed his path.

Let's Make a Deal

The town leaders had brokered a deal with the monster to keep those within the city walls safe: the monster, who was called *La Gargouille*, demanded one human from the town each year. This supplemented his diet of cattle, sheep, sailors, and those who dared to cross his territory. He had put in a request for tender young virgins as his annual treat, but the town folk just couldn't bring themselves to do that. They decided to give him prisoners who had been condemned to death instead. It didn't really change the prisoners' fate, and the monster just gobbled them right up without even noticing.

There's a New Priest in Town

The people of Rouen were gripped by fear and afraid to venture outside the town walls. Then young Father Romain arrived. The town's new priest was full of enthusiasm and faith. He felt sure he could deliver the people from their tormentor.

When the day came to feed the dragon his annual human sacrifice, brave Father Romain and a nervous prisoner headed toward the marsh where *La Gargouille* lived. The prisoner would be used as bait to lure out the monster, and if all went well and the priest captured him, the prisoner was promised a pardon.

Taming the Beast

As the faithful priest and the fearful prisoner approached *La Gargouille*'s lair, the dragon lumbered out to meet them, licking his lips and thinking that he was getting two meals this year.

He was big and ugly with thick, grey-green skin. He had wings like a bat, a long serpent-like body, and two webbed feet. His neck was long and scaly and his eyes glowed like luminescent moonstones. As he approached, the men could smell his foul breath and just as he was ready to lunge for the prisoner, Father Romain pulled out his secret weapon – a large solid gold cross that he had been holding behind his back.

As the light hit the cross and reflected into the monster's eyes, he was immediately subdued and knelt down at the priest's feet. The convict, who was holding the holy man's long scarf, gingerly tied it around the animal's neck. Then the three unlikely companions started the march back into the city: the priest leading the dragon on a leash and a very relieved criminal.

Fireproof Dragon

When they arrived at the city wall, people were amazed and terrified that the priest had brought the monster into their midst. But Father Romain assured them they were safe. They tied up *La Gargouille*, who offered no resistance, and

Romain pronounced him guilty of his many crimes. As punishment, he was to be burned at the stake.

All was prepared and the dragon was set alight in front of the church. But when the fire had burned out, *La Gargouille's* head and neck remained – they weren't even scorched. The ashes from the monster's body were thrown into the river, and his head and neck were mounted on the new church as a reminder of the power of God.

Gurgling Gargoyles

When it rained, water once again poured out the dragon's mouth, and some architect got the idea that this would be the perfect way to keep rainwater from running down the sides of the church and damaging the masonry. He carved similar dragon heads of stone and placed them all around the church. They were called gargoyles after *La Gargouille*, the river monster conquered by Father Romain. The gargoyle gutter system spread all over France and then all over the world. This is how *La Gargouille* who had threatened to destroy the town of Rouen by water came to protect church buildings from water damage all over France.

I love the rain - it reminds me of the good old days.

Pardoning Prisoners

And the prisoner who was almost the gargoyle's dinner? He started a tradition too.

Just as the priest promised, he was pardoned for his crime. To honor and remember the condemned prisoner who helped save the town, Rouen applied to the king for permission to free one condemned prisoner per year. It was granted and called the Privilege of Saint Romain.

Every year, 36 days after Easter Sunday, just before the day of Ascension, the church leaders would get together, start to interview prisoners, and listen to testimony before choosing the convict to be pardoned. On Ascension morning, they would vote, then go to collect the lucky prisoner. There would be a procession through the town in which the pardoned criminal carried the relics of Saint Romain. He would apologize for his crime, promise to never do it again, and be given official papers confirming his pardon. This pardoning tradition was abolished during the French Revolution.

Saint Romain

The plucky priest who dared to face *La Gargouille* later became Saint Romain. He is recognized in paintings and sculptures by his ever-present gargoyle on a leash.

While Saint Romain is a lesser-known saint and the pardoned prisoner is completely anonymous, everyone has heard of a gargoyle. So it seems that *La Gargouille* has the last laugh after all – especially when it's raining and he gets to spit water down on the unsuspecting people below.

~

Gargoyles and Grotesques

Technically, a gargoyle is the part of a gutter, usually in the form of a beast or sometimes of a man, that directs water away from the building. A similar carving that does not carry water is called a grotesque.

Gargoyles and Gurgles

Gargouille is the French word for gargoyle.

Gargouillement is the French word for a gurgling sound.

Once when I went to see my French doctor with a chest infection, I wanted to tell him that when I breathed there was a gurgling sound in my chest. Instead, I told him there was a gargoyle in my chest. I realized my mistake when I saw the amused look on his face. Oops! The perils of the French language...

THE MAN WHO SOLD THE EIFFEL TOWER

*I*t was 1925 and Victor Lustig was sitting in his Paris hotel room reading a newspaper article about the Eiffel Tower. That gigantic structure had been built for the 1889 Paris World's Fair and was meant to be dismantled in 1909. But because of its height, it was used as a radio tower and came in very handy for listening in on the Germans during the First World War. Now, however, it was rusting and in need of expensive repairs and maintenance. The article said the State was having difficulty finding the money for its upkeep, and the journalist ended by asking whether it might not be better just to sell it.

An Idea is Born

As Victor read this, his eyes lit up. That was it! He would sell the Eiffel Tower! Never mind that it didn't belong to him – that was just a minor detail. He had been looking for his next project and this was perfect.

Victor Lustig was born in what is now the Czech Republic. His family was well-off and he received a good education, learning to speak at least five languages. But Victor's greatest pleasure came from swindling people through the use of his abundant charm. After his schooling he was arrested for some minor crimes and then he started working on the ships that sailed between New York and Paris.

By working, I mean scamming people, of course. He would sell them boxes that printed $100 bills. These money-makers cost between $20,000 and $30,000. He would stock them with a few counterfeit $100 bills which would then very slowly emerge from the box as if they were being printed. Since it took about six hours to "print" one bill, by the time the two or three bills in the box were finished "printing," Victor would be long gone.

However, that game was starting to bore him. He was looking for something new and exciting – and selling the Eiffel Tower was just the ticket.

Make it Look Real

He went to work right away. He got stationery printed that appeared to be from the Department of Post, Telegraph and Telephone, the government department in charge of public buildings. Then he got himself a fake ID. He sent letters to the top five iron salvage companies in Paris advising them that they had been given the honor of bidding on an important government project. They were invited to a meeting at the Crillon Hotel, which had a reputation as a place where diplomatic and political deals were done. It all looked very official.

On the appointed day, the five company representatives arrived. Victor gave a convincing presentation, reiterating the well-publicized condition of the tower and the problem of maintenance and upkeep costs. Because of this, he said, the government had no choice but to dismantle and sell the tower. However, it was a potentially controversial action and required the utmost discretion. All parties agreed to keep the government's secret.

After treating them all to lunch, Victor put the five candidates in a limousine and took them to the tower for a look. A crew of workmen happened to be there measuring and assessing the tower for paint and repairs. That posed no problem for Victor who told his bamboozled band the crew was there to make preparation to dismantle the 7,000 tons of iron. He flashed his fake ID at the entrance and took his group directly in to inspect the merchandise. He informed the men that time was of the essence and he would expect their bids the next day.

Picking his Mark

In Victor's years of scamming people, he had learned to read them pretty well and he had identified his victim almost immediately. He had chosen André Poisson. Mr. Poisson was unsure of himself but eager to make his mark in Paris industry. When Mr. Poisson came in for his second meeting, he confessed that his wife had some doubts and he wasn't sure if he should go ahead with the bid.

Victor decided to put Mr. Poisson at ease by taking him into his confidence. He said that he was just an underpaid government employee. He entertained important clients in luxury, but in fact, he needed a bit of extra cash and if Mr. Poisson could add just a bit of extra padding, Victor could guarantee him the contract. Since Mr. Poisson knew that government officials were corrupt and that a con man would never ask for a bribe, he was convinced that all was legit. Mr. Poisson (whose name means "fish" in French) took the bait – he paid the asking price plus the bribe.

As soon as Victor got his suitcase full of money, he was on a train to Vienna. There he watched the newspapers every day expecting to see his masterful scam on the front page. He waited and waited, but there was nothing.

When poor Mr. Poisson had gone to the Post, Telegraph and Telephone headquarters with his bill of sale to ask when the tower would be dismantled, they laughed him out of the office. He was so embarrassed about being duped and so afraid of ruining his reputation in the city, that he didn't mention it to anyone else – not even the police.

Do It Again!

When Victor realized what had happened, he headed back to Paris to resell that tall, iron tower. He sent out five more letters to different salvage companies and repeated the entire process. This time, however, the prospective buyer did a bit more checking, found out it was a scam, and went to the police. Victor escaped just in time but without the proceeds from the second sale.

Sold for 100,000 francs to Monsieur Poisson!

Victor Lustig Auction

(But don't worry - if you didn't get it today, come back next week and I'll sell it again.)

He went to the United States where he resumed his counterfeiting activities and selling his money printing boxes. But the law eventually caught up with Victor and he was sent to Alcatraz prison, where he even conned Al Capone.

Supposedly, Victor kept a postcard of the Eiffel Tower taped on his cell wall with the words "sold for 100,000 francs" written across it. When Victor died of pneumonia in 1947, his death certificate listed his occupation as "salesman" - a tribute to his greatest scam.

MOULIN ROUGE

The Moulin Rouge is an iconic building set on the hill of Montmartre overlooking Paris. You can't miss it because there is a big red windmill on top of it, from which it takes its name. In French *moulin* means "mill," or in this case "windmill," and *rouge* is "red."

This unusual building was built in 1889, the same year as the Eiffel Tower (which Victor Lustig tried to sell). Both these buildings were products of the Belle Époque: a time when Paris was filled with innovative designs and ideas.

The Moulin Rouge was built as a place of entertainment for all classes: a place where everyone could mingle. It offered risqué cabaret shows, funny acts, and serious music. There was something for everyone. It became best known for the can-can dance with its fast, bouncy rhythms and skimpily-clad dancers.

Why a Windmill?

It was a nice idea to build a place of entertainment for the masses, but why put a big red windmill on top of it? It could be that the owners wanted to remember the roots of Montmartre. At one time this area was a rural village just outside the walls of Paris, where around 30 windmills dotted the landscape.

The Moulin Rouge was built as a mill of amusement and never ground any flour. However, two of the original Montmartre windmills are still standing, although no longer in use: the Moulin Radet and the Moulin de la Galette (formerly Butte-à-fin). In 1809 these two windmills were working mills owned by the Debray family. Then came the war of 1814. On 30 March Paris was taken by the allied Russian, Austrian, and Prussian armies.

The men of Montmartre took up arms to defend their families, their homes, and their mills. Among them were the Debray brothers. These four brothers and the oldest one's son stood their ground when the Russian army marched up the Montmartre hill. The fighting was fierce and the three youngest brothers were killed.

When word of the cease-fire reached Montmartre the oldest brother and his son were still fighting at the base of their windmill. With the announcement of the armistice, each side withdrew. But Debray was crazy with grief at losing his three brothers and he wanted revenge. He let loose a volley of bullets on the Russian troops killing a few of them.

The Russians charged the French men and rounded them all up. The commanding officer demanded that the person responsible for firing on his troops step forward. If not, he would kill everyone. The remaining Debray brother stepped forward and the commander shot him then and there.

The Russians wanted to make a point, so they cut Debray's body into four pieces and hung them on the four blades of the windmill. That night, one of the Debray women took down the body parts, put them in flour sacks and took them to the cemetery. The next day the French surrendered and Napoleon was forced into exile on Elba Island.

The oldest brother's son survived. Even though he was run through with a sword, he lived to tell the tale. His stomach, however, was never the same and he could only drink milk from then on. After he recovered, he turned his two wind-mills into drinking establishments. He added a dance floor to one and called it Le Moulin de la Galette. Legend says that milk was the only drink served there.

The Debray Family tomb is in the cemetery Saint-Pierre du Calvaire de Montmartre. There is a windmill on the tomb and some say it was painted red at one time. Could the red windmill of the Moulin Rouge be a tribute to the brave Debray men?

In 1889 when Charles Zidler and Joseph Oller designed the Moulin Rouge building with a windmill on the top, it was a nod to the past and the rich historical association of Mont-martre with its windmills.

THE MAD FARTER

*W*hen you mention the Moulin Rouge, most people think of its can-can dancers. But do you know who was their highest paid performer at the end of the nineteenth century? His name was Joseph Pujol and he had a very peculiar talent. He could fart on demand and in various tones, even playing songs.

Monsieur Pujol, who was born in Marseille, France in 1857, had the unusual ability to take in air (or water) at will through his bottom. Then through muscle control he was able to regulate the speed and force of the expulsion. He first discovered that his posterior was different from those of other young men one summer when he went swimming in the sea. As he was preparing to plunge his head underwater, he took a deep breath and contracted his abdominal muscles. Suddenly he felt his insides fill with cold water. Of course, he was terrified and rushed to the shore. He and others were amazed as he stood on the beach with water pouring out of his behind like a fire hose. The doctor examined him and assured him that he was fine. So, as any teenage boy would, he started to practice and develop his newfound talent.

The Human Water Fountain

Joseph was born to perform. Even as a child, he would sing, dance and play trombone for visitors to his parents' home. So it was only natural that he wanted to show off his newly discovered skill every chance he got. During his time in the army, he further developed his talents while entertaining his comrades-in-arms. He would imitate a fountain, taking in water through his bum and then shooting it high into the air. Soon he discovered that his ability wasn't limited to water. He could also inhale and exhale air through his bottom. This allowed him to enlarge his repertoire by adding "music" and impressions.

It was in the army that Joseph acquired the nickname that would later become his stage name. He was called *Le Pétomane* which came from two French words: *péter* (to fart) and *maniaque*. This translates to something like "The Mad Farter."

Musical Career

After the army, Joseph returned to Marseille where he worked as a baker, often entertaining customers with his "other talents." However, he yearned for a larger audience, so he left the bakery and took to the stage with his trombone. It didn't take long for him to discover that the audience preferred his other wind instrument. His flatulent act became a big hit in Marseille, and he decided to take it to Paris.

In Paris, the Moulin Rouge, which had just been open for a few years, was eager to put him under contract – and a windmill seemed just the place for his windy act. He was an instant success and people laughed so hard during his performances that some passed out – especially the women who were strapped into their corsets so tightly that when they went into fits of laughter, they could no longer breathe. Nurses had to be on duty in the theatre when *Le Pétomane* was performing to take care of those who fainted from having too much fun.

You all know this one.
Now sing along with me!

A Fartistic Show

Monsieur Pujol would appear on stage in his suit looking quite sophisticated. He would explain to the audience that the wind he was about to produce was completely odorless and that no one could say his show was a stinker. Then he went on to entertain them with imitations of thunderstorms, cannons, and simple musical renditions. Later in the act, he would step offstage and connect a long tube to his *derrière* through a special discreet opening in the back of his trousers. Using this tube he would smoke two cigarettes at once – one with his mouth and one through his... tube. He would also blow out candles from an impressive distance before attaching a small flute to the tube to play more tunes.

To prove that there was no trickery, he gave special performances (for men only) in his underwear which was fitted with a hole in the back large enough for the men to verify that the performance was real. He also gave private performances to those who didn't want to be seen publicly enjoying his low-brow humor, such as the Prince of Wales (the future English king Edward VII) and King Leopold II of Belgium.

Trouble at the Windmill

During the two years he was at the Moulin Rouge (1892-1894), he was a great success, even earning a higher fee than Sarah Bernhardt. But this all came to an end when, at the request of a friend, Joseph gave a performance at a fair. The Moulin Rouge saw this as a breach of contract and took him to court. When Joseph lost the case and had to pay damages, he and the red windmill parted ways.

The Moulin Rouge had won the case, but they had lost their biggest money-maker. They soon replaced Joseph by a female version of *Le Pétomane*. However, unlike Joseph, her talent was not a natural gift. She had a concealed bellows-like device beneath her skirts. Joseph was furious when he heard of this and he went back to court, this time to accuse the Moulin Rouge of trickery. He was declared the only true *pétomane* when the imposter was exposed.

Joseph was vindicated and went on to open his own theatre where he performed his flatulent act for another 20 years. Then in 1914, when the First World War broke out, he retired from the stage and returned to Marseille. At first he worked in a bakery and later bought a biscuit factory in Toulon.

He died in 1945 at the age of 88 near Toulon. Even after all those years, his special talent had not been forgotten and a Parisian medical school offered to buy his body so they could study his curious anatomy. The family refused and he rests today in the cemetery of La Valette-du-Var.

LIKE WHAT YOU'VE READ?

LEAVE A REVIEW

I hope you've enjoyed this collection of stories about France. If you have, I would really appreciate it if you would leave a review on Amazon, Goodreads, or whichever bookstore you bought it through. Reviews help potential readers decide whether or not a book is for them. They also help authors by giving their books credibility and make them more visible in the marketplace.

Thank you in advance.

ABOUT MARGO

I'm American by birth, but feel at home in Europe after years of living in the UK and France. Life is never dull here with so much history to discover. There's a story hiding around every corner and I'm always trying to find it.

I'm curious by nature and I'm forever wanting to know who, what, why, when, where, and how... When I find answers to these questions, I share them on my blog, the Curious Rambler, or in my Curious Histories books. (Are you beginning to notice a curious theme?)

I share my adventures (and my questions) with Jeff, my husband of many years. I enjoy travel, history, observing cultures and traditions - and then writing about them, of course.

~

You can follow me on my website: curiousrambler.com (Curious Rambler).

Thank you for reading.

Printed in Great Britain
by Amazon

75232341R00086